Smallta

Best Practice

Patterns

Kent Beck

To join a Prentice Hall Internet mailing list,
point to http://www.prenhall.com/register.

Prentice Hall PTR, Upper Saddle River, New Jersey 07458

Library of Congress Cataloging-in-Publication Data

Beck, Kent.

    Smalltalk best practice patterns / Kent Beck.

       p. cm.

    Includes index.

    ISBN 0-13-476904-X (pbk.)

    1. Smalltalk (Computer program language) I. Title.

QA76.73.S59B43 1997

005.13'3--dc20   96-29411

                                         CIP

Editorial/Production Supervision: *Joe Czerwinski*
Acquisitions Editor: *Paul Becker*
Editorial Assistant: *Maureen Diana*
Manufacturing Manager: *Alexis R. Heydt*
Cover Design Director: *Jerry Votta*
Cover Design: *Design Source*

©1997 by Prentice Hall PTR
Prentice-Hall, Inc.
A Division of Simon and Schuster
Upper Saddle River, NJ 07458

The publisher offers discounts on this book when ordered
in bulk quantities. For more information, contact:

    Corporate Sales Department
    Prentice Hall PTR
    One Lake Street
    Upper Saddle River, NJ 07458

    Phone: 800-382-3419
    Fax: 201-236-7141
    E-mail: corpsales@prenhall.com

Printed in the United States of America

10 9 8 7 6 5 4 3 2

ISBN: 0-13-476904-X

Prentice-Hall International (UK) Limited, *London*
Prentice-Hall of Australia Pty. Limited, *Sydney*
Prentice-Hall of Canada Inc., *Toronto*
Prentice-Hall Hispanoamericana, S.A., *Mexico*
Prentice-Hall of India Pte. Ltd., *New Delhi*
Prentice-Hall of Japan, Inc., *Tokyo*
Simon & Schuster Asia Pte. Ltd., *Singapore*
Editora Prentice-Hall do Brasil, Ltda., *Rio de Janeiro*

Contents

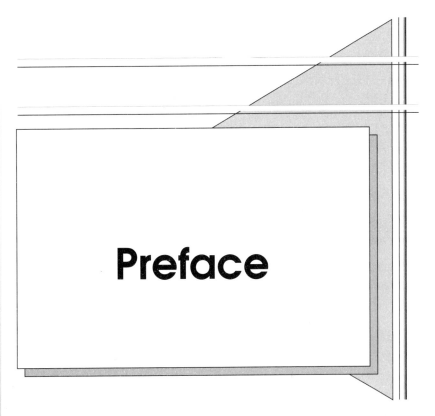

Preface

This preface will explain what this book is about. It will convince you to buy this book, or you will know why you shouldn't (more of the former than the latter, I hope).

What's it all about?

This book is about the simple things experienced, successful Smalltalkers do that beginners don't. In a sense, it is a style guide. I have tried to penetrate beneath the surface, though, to get at the human realities that make the rules work instead of focusing solely on the rules themselves.

The topics covered are the daily tactics of programming:

- How do you choose names for objects, variables, and methods?

- How do you break logic into methods?

- How do you communicate most clearly through your code?

These are small scale issues. There are also many bigger technical reasons why projects fail (and many more nontechnical reasons).

The attraction of this set of issues is that they are so tractable. You don't have to be a programming wizard to pick good names, you just have to have good advice.

The advice is broken into 92 patterns. Each pattern presents:

- a recurring daily programming problem;
- the tradeoffs that affect solutions to the problem; and
- a concrete recipe to create a solution for the problem.

For example, here is a summary of a pattern called "Role Suggesting Temporary Variable Name":

Problem: What do you name a temporary variable?

Tradeoffs:

- You want to include lots of information in the name.
- You want the name to be short so it is easy to type and doesn't make formatting difficult.
- You don't want redundant information in the name.
- You want to communicate why the variable exists.
- You want to communicate the type of the variable (i.e. what messages it is sent).

Solution: Name the variable after the role it plays. The type can be inferred from context, and so doesn't need to be part of the name.

You will see in the body of the book that each pattern occupies a page or two. Each pattern includes examples (and counter-examples) from the standard Smalltalk images. Each pattern also talks about related patterns.

The patterns don't stand in isolation, 92 independent bits of advice. Patterns work together, leading you from larger problems to smaller. Together they form a system or language. The system, as a whole, allows you to focus on the problem at hand, confident that tomorrow you can deal with tomorrow's problems.

Why should you read it?

Learning—If you are just learning Smalltalk, these patterns will give you a big jump start on making effective use of the system. Because the patterns aren't just rules, you can smoothly go from merely following the patterns, to understanding why they are the way they are, to formulating your own patterns. You will need a good basic introduction to Smalltalk in addition to this book, but reading them together will greatly accelerate your learning.

Programming—If you program in Smalltalk, these patterns will give you a catalog of techniques that work well. You will have discovered or invented many of them yourself, but the patterns may give you a fresh perspective on why they work or present nuances you hadn't considered.

Teaching—If you teach Smalltalkers, either as a mentor or in classroom training, these patterns will give you large bag of instructional material. If you are trying to explain why code should be different, it is much more satisfying for you and the learner to be able to discuss the pattern and how it applies to the particular situation.

Managing—If you manage Smalltalk projects, you may be struggling with how to apply good software engineering principles to Smalltalk. These patterns don't address that topic directly, but they can become the basis of a common vocabulary for your developers.

What isn't it about?

This is not a book of methodology. It will not guide your entire development process. You can use it with your existing process, whether you invented it or it came out of a book. This book is about making code that works for you.

This is not a book of philosophy. If you want to understand what makes programs good in the abstract, if you want to learn to write patterns yourself, or understand their philosophical or psychological basis, you won't find any help here. This book is for people who have programs to write and want to do so as quickly, safely, and effectively as possible.

This is not a book of design. If design is the process of defining the relationships among small families of objects, the resulting problems repeat just as surely as do implementation problems. Design patterns are very effective at capturing that commonality. They just aren't the topic of this book. This book is about making Smalltalk work for you. Making objects work for you is an entirely different topic.

Acknowledgments

I would like to thank the many people who contributed to this volume. First I would like to thank the Xerox PARC Learning Research Group (Alan Kay, Adele Goldberg, Dan Ingalls, Diana Merry-Shapiro, Ted Kaehler, Larry Tesler, and Bob Flegel) for having the insights in the first place, so I had something to write down. I would like to thank my mentor and intellectual partner, Ward Cunningham, for showing me the way and sharing his insights. Many of the patterns here he identified and/or named. Thanks to my reviewers (Dirk Riehle, David N. Smith, Mitchell Model, Bill Reynolds, Dave Smith, Trygve

Reenskaug, Ralph Johnson, John Brant, Don Roberts, Brian Foote, Brian Marick, Joe Yoder, Ian Chai, Mark Kendrat, Eric Scouten, Charles Herring, Haidong Ye, Kevin Powell, Rob Brown, Kyle Brown, Bobby Woolf, Harald Mueller, Steve Hayes, Bob Biros, David Warren, Gert Florijn, Mark L. Fussell, Martin Fowler, Chuck Siska, Chris Bird, Ron Jefferies, Volker Wurst, Peter Epstein, Thomas Murphy, Michel Brassard, Ron Jefferies, John Sellers, Steve Messick, Darrow Kirkpatrick, Phoenix Tong, Doug Lea, Randy Stafford, Sharry Fealk and all the reviewers who didn't put their names on their comments) for reading early rough drafts carefully. Finally, this book would never have been finished without my ever patient but gently prodding editor, Paul Becker.

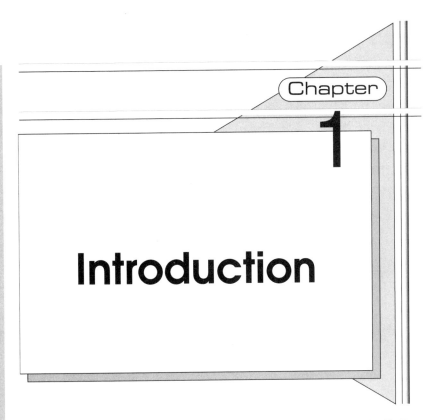

Introduction

Let's start by taking a close look at the title: *Smalltalk Best Practice Patterns*. That's a mouthful. What does it mean?

Smalltalk—That part is easy. I assume you know at least something about Smalltalk or you wouldn't be reading this book.

Best Practice—Best practice is a legal term. Looked at positively, best practice is the set of procedures and skills that professionals recognize and use. Looked at negatively, if you can prove that you were using the current best practice when you did a piece of work, you can't be sued for negligence. I prefer to look at it positively. At least, I hope this book is never held up in court!

Patterns—A pattern is a decision an expert makes over and over. For example, naming an instance variable after the role it plays is a pattern. Even though all the results (in this case, all the variable names) are different, they have a quality that is constant. The heart of this book is 92 such patterns.

Coding

I'd like to say a bit about coding to give you a clearer idea of the activities covered by the patterns.

1

When computers were the province of the physics department or the math department, there was no such thing as coding as a separate activity. People had ideas, they implemented them, they looked at the results.

Developer castes appeared with the advent of commercial software development. At the top were the systems analysts, lofty intellects too important to actually use computers. Below them were the programmers, who knew how to turn the vague mutterings of the analysts into something the assembler or (later) compiler could recognize. At the bottom were coders, who took the sheets, filled out by the programmers, and created punched cards.

Better interface technology has long rendered the coder-as-typist obsolete. The word has come to mean all the low level activities of programming. The stigma remains, however. When I became a consultant, I was told, "Don't let them know you can code, or you'll never be able to charge premium rates."

I think the time has come for a redefinition of coding. Not really redefinition, I suppose, but a rehabilitation. I like the definition just fine. I think the stigma attached to it is short-sighted and dangerous.

To me, development consists of two processes that feed each other. First, you figure out what you want the computer to do. Then, you instruct the computer to do it. Trying to write those instructions inevitably changes what you want the computer to do, and so it goes.

In this model, coding isn't the poor handmaiden of design or analysis. Coding is where your fuzzy, comfortable ideas awaken in the harsh dawn of reality. It is where you learn what your computer can do. If you stop coding, you stop learning.

We aren't always good at guessing where responsibilities should go. Coding is where our design guesses are tested. Being prepared to be flexible about making design changes during coding results in programs that get better and better over time. Insisting that early design ideas be carried through is short sighted. Often, I see some ugly code in an object. Based on the patterns in this book (most often Composed Method), I'll suggest that the code be moved to another object. For example, I saw code that looked like this:

```
Station>>computePart: aPart
    ^self multiplyPartTimesRate: aPart
Station>>multiplyPartTimesRate: aPart
    ^Part
        amount: aPart amount * self rate
        date: aPart date
```

I said, "we seem to be using a lot of the Part's data in multiplyPartTimesRate:. Why don't we move this code into Part?" "But we didn't design Parts to do arithmetic!" "Since the code seems to be telling us to do this, let's try it."

```
Part>>* aRate
    ^Part
            amount: amount * aRate
            date: date
Station>>computePart: aPart
    ^aPart * self rate
```

The result is simpler, shorter, and exposes less of a Part's details to the Station. Being open to design insights during coding, we learned something that made our whole system simpler.

My inspiration for the material in this book is my experience reviewing code. As I write, I remember more and more incidents, "Oh, yeah. That client was doing that wrong and it was really killing them. What can I say about that?" The advice I give in such situations is tactical, coding advice of necessity. I don't have time for a deep understanding of their problem. I'm constantly amazed at how even a little help cleaning up small problems reveals the source and solution of much bigger problems.

Talking Programs

Did you know that your program talks to you? I don't mean those "Buy more Jolt Cola" messages. I mean important stuff about how your system ought to be structured.

If you're programming along, doing nicely, and all of a sudden your program gets balky, makes things hard for you, it's talking. It's telling you there is something important missing.

Many of the patterns tell you what to do when your program talks to you. Sometimes you need to create a new method, sometimes a new object, sometimes a new variable. Whatever the needed response, you have to be listening before you can react.

As programmers, we have all been through terrible experiences with systems that seemed designed to make life difficult (this word processor, for instance). It is easy to get numbed to pain and frustration, or treat it as if it were part of the territory. Your programs don't have to be like that. You can make them clean and simple and easy to read.

"It looks like we need to put this over here."

"We can't do that. That's not how it works."

"Wait a minute. The code would be easier to read and more flexible if we did it this way."

"But that's not what that object does."

"Let's just do it and see if we like it."

...murmel, murmel, murmel...

"Hey, that is better."

I can't begin to count how many times I've been through this scenario. The good news is, it's not that I'm any smarter than my clients or that I can see how to improve code where they can't. It's just that I know what to pay attention to (what patterns to look for) and I have the confidence to simply follow where the code leads.

Some of the biggest improvements come from figuring out how to eliminate:

- Duplicate code (even little bits of it)
- Conditional logic
- Complex methods
- Structural code (where one object treats another as a data structure)

These patterns will give you a toolbox of problems to look for and ways to fix them. As time goes on, you'll find yourself creating fewer and fewer problems in the first place. I hope you get better than me, though, at writing patterns correctly the first time. I still get myself into a pickle far too often.

Good Software

The patterns here form a system; one that I have developed during my years as a Smalltalk programmer. Most of it is really the work of the Smalltalkers who came before me and left their wisdom in the image. Some small part is my own invention. I consider myself part of a culture. As with any culture, there is a core set of values that drives what the culture sees as good and what it sees as bad. What are those values?

Well, what makes a good program? There are, of course, lots of definitions of what makes a good program, and even lots of valid definitions. In telecommunications or medical instrumentation, an absolutely reliable program is a good program. In derivatives trading, a quickly shipped program is a good program.

Most commercial software isn't so extreme. The life of most programs goes like this:

1. It is developed in a hurry by a team of developers. Time to market is critical for reducing the business risk of a new product. The product itself is technically challenging to build but doesn't break new ground in lots of areas at once.

2. The product lives for several years, during which time its capabilities are refined and extended, often by developers who weren't part of the original team.

3. Bits and pieces of the product are cannibalized for new projects, again, not by the original developers.

A good program balances the needs of these activities. No one phase can be allowed to dominate the others without risking the business viability of a system.

Sometimes, you will find a pattern supports all the phases—you will be able to develop code faster, with less risk and have it be easier to maintain and reuse. Often, though, you have to rob Peter to pay Paul. Most of the patterns are designed to preserve a balance between short-term and long-term needs.

I can't say it often enough—the bottlenecks throughout development come from limitations in human communication. Over and over in the patterns, you will read "You could do this or you could do that, but this over here communicates best, so that's what you should do." If there's a radical thought here, that's it; that when you program, you have to think about how someone will read your code, not just how a computer will interpret it.

Here are the criteria I considered in writing these patterns, and the accommodation I made to them.

-   Productivity—You can spend productivity gains any way you'd like—shorter time to market, reduced development cost, reduced technical risk, or improved quality. I wrote the patterns so developers of all skill levels could learn more quickly and spend less time on the mechanics of engineering good software in Smalltalk.

-   Lifecycle Cost—If there is one driving force behind these patterns, it is the reduction of the lifecycle costs of software. Too many development organizations get into a deadly embrace with their own projects, where they are spending so much time and energy just keeping the last system alive and limping that they can't meet the needs of today's market, much less tomorrow's. I wrote the patterns so they could be taught to developers and maintainers, used day to day in development and documentation, so that throughout the life of a project it remains easy to enhance.

- Time to Market—When pressure become intense to get a product to market, it is tempting to cut corners. However, the very act of deciding what corners to cut slows down development. Using these patterns lets you program flat out, applying patterns as fast as your fingers will go, and get results as quickly as possible, without paying an exorbitant cost in the long run.

- Risk—Risk is the great taboo in software. Everybody knows that lots of projects fail. Everybody knows that you can't really schedule software development reliably and still produce interesting products. Everybody knows that software development is risky, but nobody talks about it. When I review a project at risk, I am amazed at how often the big picture is in place, but a slew of little mistakes are gumming up the works. I wrote these patterns from my experience of seeing which little things most often hurt projects.

Style

Good programming style is one of those things that everyone knows when they see it but is very hard to articulate precisely. The capitalist's cant—a good programming style is one that makes money—is objectively measurable but hard to apply day to day.

There are a few things I look for that are good predictors of whether a project is in good shape. These are also properties I strive for in my code.

- Once and only once—If I only have one minute to describe good style, I reduce it to a simple rule: In a program written with good style, everything is said once and only once. This isn't much help in creating good code, but it's a darned good analytic tool. If I see several methods with the same logic, several objects with the same methods, or several systems with similar objects, I know this rule isn't satisfied. This leads us to the second property:

- Lots of little pieces—Good code invariably has small methods and small objects. Only by factoring the system into many small pieces of state and function can you hope to satisfy the "once and only once" rule. I get lots of resistance to this idea, especially from experienced developers, but no one thing I do to systems provides as much help as breaking it into more pieces. When you are doing this, however, you must always be certain that you communicate the big picture effectively. Otherwise, you'll find yourself in a big bowl of

"Pasta à la Smalltalk," which is every bit as nasty a dish as "Fettucine à la C."

- Replacing objects—Good style leads to easily replaceable objects. In a really good system, every time the user says "I want to do this radically different thing," the developer says, "Oh, I'll have to make a new kind of X and plug it in." When you can extend a system solely by adding new objects without modifying any existing objects, then you have a system that is flexible and cheap to maintain. You can't do this if you don't have lots of little pieces.

- Moving objects—Another property of systems with good style is that their objects can be easily moved to new contexts. You should be able to say, "This object in this system does the same job in that system." Warning—the first time you try to move an object, you will discover you have done it wrong, that it doesn't generalize well. Don't try to move it too early in the game. Ship a couple of systems first. Then, if you have a system built with lots of little pieces, you will be able to make the necessary modifications and generalizations fairly easily.

- Rates of change—A simple criteria I use all the time is checking rates of change. I learned this criteria from something Brad Cox said a long time ago. I've since generalized it to—don't put two rates of change together. Don't have part of a method that changes in every subclass with parts that don't change. Don't have some instance variables whose values change every second in the same object with instance variables whose values change once a month. Don't have a collection where some elements are added and removed every second and some elements are added and removed once a month. Don't have code in an object that has to change for every piece of hardware, and code that has to change for every operating system. How do you avoid this problem? You got it, lots of little pieces.

What's Missing?

There are a few coding topics I don't cover here; not because they aren't important, but because I don't yet understand them well enough to turn them into patterns. I hope I learn enough about them to include them in a second edition. Here are the topics I deliberately do not cover:

- Exception handling—I use exception handling as sparingly as possible, generally, only around the highest level invocation of objects from the user interface. Lots of handlers make debugging difficult, because the code just runs to completion but provides the wrong answer. When you use exception handling, you have to think like the writer of a new programming language, not just an application developer.

- Copying—Fixing bugs by making copies of objects before operating on them is nice and simple. Unfortunately, when copying becomes a habit, you can end up slowing down your system by making unnecessary copies or introducing bugs by not changing objects that need to be changed.

- Become—There are legitimate uses of become, but debugging code that uses it is so difficult already, if you have any other option for solving your problem, you're probably better off. If you are experienced enough to be an exception to this rule, then you won't be taking what I write as gospel anyway, so I'm not afraid to be doctrinaire on this point.

- Performance—Performance tuning is a whole topic unto itself. Its biggest problem in this context is that all the patterns here maximize the communication value of code. Performance tuning often sacrifices clarity for speed.

The definition of "coding" in the first section of this chapter, namely tactical programming decisions, excludes many topics. Here are some of the topics I hope to cover in future volumes:

- Design—There are a host of techniques that are just upstream (to my view) of the material covered here. They are the patterns whereby two objects can do a better job than one, or when turning a method or set of methods into an object provides leverage. For now, I will refer you to "Design Patterns" by Gamma et. al.

- Modeling—The patterns here resolve constraints imposed by Smalltalk. Many of the most important decisions you make must also resolve constraints imposed by the problem you are modeling.

- Requirements—How you agree with the client about what must be done, and more importantly what need not be done, has an enormous impact on the success of your development. If you don't do what's needed, the client will not be satisfied with the result. If you do what isn't needed, you add cost, time, and most importantly, risk to your project.

- User Interface Design and Implementation—Designing interfaces that users find valuable is an art. Implementing them simply, flexibly, and reusably is the test of a solid Smalltalker.

Book Organization

Here are the chapters:

- Patterns—The philosophy behind patterns.

- Behavior—Patterns for methods and messages. The problems you can solve by creating a new method. You will also find method patterns scattered throughout the remainder of the patterns, if a particular kind of method (like accessors) is tied to another pattern. The quick reference guide gathers all the method patterns together for easy reference.

- State—Patterns for using instance and temporary variables. You will find a discussion of the pros and cons of using accessor methods and direct variable access.

- Collections—The major collection classes and messages in the form of patterns. You will also find common tricks using collections.

- Classes—A brief introduction to how to use classes, since most of the topics regarding class creation are outside the scope of this book.

- Formatting—My rules of code formatting, cast as patterns.

- Development Example—An example of developing objects with explicit reference to the patterns, as they apply.

Adoption

How can you learn and use these patterns?

- Bag of tricks—This is the toe-dipper's approach to these patterns. If you feel like you already have a pretty good handle on Smalltalk but you want to make sure your golf bag is full of clubs, you can skim these patterns looking for new techniques. I suggest the sections on Collection Idioms and Messages as a starting point.

- Custom style guide—I've seen many development organizations, recently, where one or two experienced Smalltalkers are asked to provide leadership for a group of new Smalltalk developers. One of the first tasks of the gurus is generally to educate the troops and develop a style guide. You gurus can pick your favorite patterns from the ones presented here, add important ones that I left out, or fix ones I messed up, and use your new list as the basis for training and standards.

- Whole hog—Read the patterns through once quickly. Then set this book on your lap as you program. Every time you are about to do anything—write a method, name a variable, name a message—look it up first. When you are sure you are following a pattern, you can quit looking it up. At first, this is sure to be frustrating, and the more experience you have before you start, the more frustrating it will be.

My experience going "whole hog" was that I spent a couple of frustrating weeks programming at less than full speed. After that, I memorized enough patterns to get back up to my old productivity, but the code I was producing was cleaner than before. After a couple more weeks, I no longer had to look up any patterns, and my productivity shot up while my code kept getting cleaner and cleaner.

Why does this work? I think it is because when I used to program, I would constantly have two parallel conversations going on in my head—what should I name this variable and how should I approach naming this variable. I was always looking for exceptions to my rules, trying to gain some small advantage. When I chose to follow the patterns explicitly, that second conversation disappeared and I paid more attention to the problem I was solving.

Learning a Pattern

If you've programmed before, whether in Smalltalk or another language, you will certainly recognize some of the patterns immediately. However, some patterns will present material that is new to you, or at least present it in a way that is unfamiliar. What do you do when faced with a pattern you don't immediately understand? The following suggestions are in no particular order.

- Context—Have a look at the preceding and following patterns. Each pattern solves a small part of the problem of building good systems. Sometimes, putting a pattern in context helps you understand what part of the problem the pattern is solving.

- Example—Each pattern has an example towards the end. Look at the example and see if you can guess what rule created it. Then, check with the pattern's solution to see if your answer is the same as mine.

- Problem/Solution—I like reading the patterns just as problems and solutions. The Quick Reference Card is organized like that. The intervening material supports the pattern, but sometimes it can be distracting. Once you understand the problem and solution, the discussion may clarify your understanding.

- Look for Examples—Go through your Smalltalk image looking for examples or counter-examples to a pattern. When you see a possible example, try to understand whether the purpose of the pattern is the same as the purpose of the writer of the code.

- Try to Write an Example—Apply the pattern to some of your own code. Use your best understanding of the pattern.

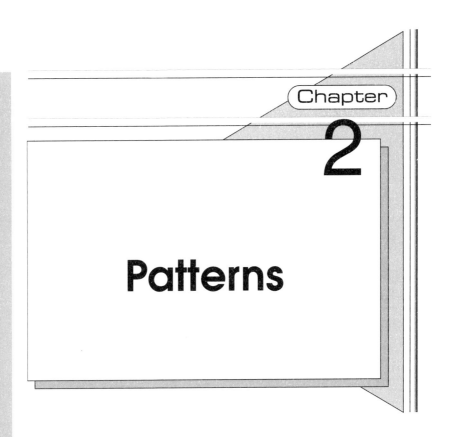

Chapter

2

Patterns

Developers don't ever develop from scratch. Many problems recur in various guises throughout development. Mature engineering disciplines capitalize on the repetitive nature of development by collecting handbooks of adequate solutions to recurring problems. A bridge designer designs using the solutions in the handbook, like I-beams, not the laws of physics.

Interest in software reuse reveals a recognition that software engineering is just as repetitious as other engineering disciplines. If leveraging the commonality in software development is the problem, though, large scale code reuse has not proven to be the answer.

Patterns form a more flexible basis for producing systematic variations on the common themes of software engineering. Each pattern records a solution to a single recurring problem, including how to recognize the presence of the problem and how to generate the solution so that it fits the context. Patterns lead naturally one to the other, forming a kind of flexible fabric of decisions that can solve large scale problems.

Why Patterns Work

Here is the Big Assumption: There are only so many things objects can do. Not in the sense that there are a limited number of applications, because there will always be new domains to model, but in the sense that the same structures of objects keep appearing over and over, regardless of the application. The problems in the construction of objects are universal. You have to name classes, relate classes via inheritance and delegation, relate methods in the same class and different classes, name variables, and so on. Patterns record these problems and how to approach solving them.

Communicating with our computers used to be the hardest thing about developing systems. It has taken years, but advances in programming languages, programming environments, and programming style have largely eliminated the barriers to instructing the computer.

When the hardest problem is solved, something else becomes the hardest problem. The next bottleneck in software engineering is human communication. When we say that 70 percent of the development budget is spent on maintenance, we mean that the poor maintainers have to wade through piles of documentation and code to discover the intent of the original programmer. The advent of widespread reuse exacerbates the problem. No longer is one maintainer the audience for one develope., Hundreds, thousands, or hundreds of thousands of elaborators are trying to understand the intent of an abstractor.

When you want to improve communication, you have two choices; either increase the bandwidth so you can communicate more bits or increase the context shared between sender and receiver so the same number of bits mean more. The first is impractical, especially in the presence of reuse (one developer can only be sliced into so many pieces), so we must find some way to make our words mean more.

When you want to optimize any process, the first strategy to employ is to find how the common case is simpler than the general case. For software engineering, the general case is the programming language. Commonly, though, we don't go all the way back to the programming language to solve problems. We look at what we did last week and last year, and what our friends did last week and last year, and do something similar.

Small, tightly knit development organizations demonstrate the cumulative effects of this kind of optimization. Because everyone shares the same experiences, a simple word or phrase takes on a big meaning. "I've got this problem, how am I going to solve it?" "Well, you could try that graphics editor trick." "Exactly. That should work great." Small organizations become dramatically more productive when they gather a critical mass of these "catch phrases."

There are two problems with relying on an oral tradition to transmit this information. First, members of the team become almost incomprehensible to someone not initiated into the dialect. Second, the process doesn't scale. The team can't grow big without losing the benefits of its private language, and one team's experience can't transfer easily to another.

Patterns are a literary form for capturing and transmitting common practice. Each pattern records a recurring problem, how to construct a solution for the problem, and why the solution is appropriate. By carrying along their justification, patterns avoid the problem of most "style guides" that simply prescribe solutions without discussing why or when the solution is appropriate. If you are faced with the recurring problem named in a pattern, after you read the pattern, you should be convinced that the solution called for in the pattern is appropriate—or you should know why it isn't.

Patterns exist and can be articulated at all levels of development. There are patterns that tell you how to schedule and sequence system development, how to create an application with a particular class library, how to design new objects, and how to format source code so that it communicates as clearly as possible.

Individual patterns become valuable when they are woven together to form a sort of flexible recipe for development. Expertise in development often hinges on knowing what problems should be solved first and what problems can be safely ignored. When each pattern names patterns that precede and complete it, the result is a rich language for capturing software engineering expertise.

Role of Patterns

Reading

These patterns are used (sometimes not in precisely the form they appear here) in the construction of the Smalltalk images sold by the vendors. Early in your Smalltalking career, you will spend most of your time reading code from the image. If you know what to expect and you understand why the code is the way it is, you will be able to read and understand more quickly and thoroughly.

Development

During development, you will run into the same Smalltalk problems over and over. You can use these patterns as a guide for how to solve these problems. "What should I name this instance variable?" —flip to Role Suggesting

Instance Variable Name and follow the solution. After you use a pattern a few times, you will internalize it, so you won't have to go continuously looking up the details. You can put the quick reference guide up so you don't have to program with this whole book on your lap.

Review

Group reviews will go much more smoothly if everyone knows and uses the patterns. You can use the patterns to point out opportunities for improvement in code—"I see, you need a Constructor Method for that class so these three methods can be simpler."

Documentation

You can describe a system using patterns much more simply than if you use ordinary prose. A few words can take the place of many paragraphs and do a better job because so much is implied by the patterns. If I say, "#x:y: and #r:theta: are the Constructor Methods for Point," you know exactly what I am talking about (or will when you read Constructor Method on page 23).

Clean Up

When I am consulting, I clean up code using the patterns as a way of both understanding what is there and preparing for making quick changes once I understand what's wrong and what's required. I generally start with the formatting patterns (page 171), then simplify methods with Composed Method (page 21) and Explaining Temporary Variable (page 108). Once I am done with this, it is easy to see where there is duplicated code, the sign of an opportunity for improvement.

Format

Each pattern records an atomic decision made repeatedly by experienced Smalltalk developers. They are written so you can follow them almost blindly, as just "good advice." As your understanding matures, each pattern gives you enough information that you can begin to delve into the "why" of the pattern. After you have used a pattern enough, you should begin to understand its limitations and when you should break the rule.

Each pattern has the same format, so you can quickly scan them when you are looking for a solution to a particular problem. The following elements appear in every pattern:

Element	Purpose
Title	Names the thing created as a result of executing the pattern. Intended to be used conversationally to refer to the pattern— "Oh, I think you need a State Object here."
Preceding patterns	Briefly describes which pattern precedes this one and why. Some patterns are nonsense taken out of order. Other orderings are the result of experience about which problems are most important and which can be safely deferred. ***Appears in Avant Garde Bold Italic.***
Problem	Stated as a question. Reading the problem will quickly tell you whether you are interested in the rest of the pattern. Appears in Avant Garde.
Forces	Describes the constraints on any solution to the problem and argues for the solution called for in this pattern. After reading the forces section, you should either be convinced that the solution is valid for your situation or you should know why the solution isn't valid. Sometimes it takes the form of a description of alternatives and why they don't work, sometimes it's just a discussion of the influences on the design decision.
Solution	Gives you an unambiguous, concrete recipe for creating the thing named by the title of the pattern. These will typically be development environment actions—subclass this, name this variable thus-and-so, etc. *Appears in Avant Garde Italic.*
Discussion	Tells you how to make practical use of the pattern. May contain an example of use or give you issues to watch out for. Appears in Avant Garde.
Following patterns	Tells you what patterns should be considered next. ***Appears in Avant Garde Bold Italic.***

You can learn a lot about the patterns by just reading the titles, problems, and solutions. Indeed, that is what the quick reference card contains. When you want to go beyond the simple recipes, though, you will need to study the forces section and the links between patterns to understand their intent.

Behavior

Objects model the world through behavior and state. Behavior is the dynamic, active, computational part of the model. State is what is left after behavior is done, how the model is represented before, after, and during a computation.

Of the two, behavior is the more important to get right. The primacy of behavior is one of the odd truths of objects; odd because it flies in the face of so much accumulated experience. Back in the bad old days, you wanted to get the representation right as quickly as possible because every change to the representation bred changes in many different computations.

Objects (done right) change all that. No longer is your system a slave of its representation. Because objects can hide their representation behind a wall of messages, you are free to change representation and only affect one object.

Behavior in systems of objects is specified in two ways; with messages and methods. I saw a great comment at OOPSLA (the Object Oriented Programming Languages, Systems and Applications conference). It said, "This seems an awful fuss for a fancy procedure call." Well, separating computation into messages and methods and binding the message to the method at run time, based on the class of the receiver, may seem like a small change from an ordinary procedure call, but it is a small change that makes a big difference.

This section tells you how to specify behavior so that your intent is clearly communicated to your reader. Many constraints affect your choices when specifying behavior. The more centralized the flow of control, the easier it is to follow in the sense that you don't have to go bouncing around all over the place to understand how work is accomplished. However, centralizing control kills flexibility. You want to have lots of objects involved so you have many opportunities to replace objects to change the system, and so you can completely factor code.

Methods

Methods are important to the system because they are how work gets done in Smalltalk. Just as important, methods are the way you communicate to readers how you intended for work to get done. You must write your methods with both of these audiences in mind. Methods must do the work they are supposed to do but they must also communicate the intent of the work to be done.

Methods decompose the function of your program into easily digestible chunks. Carefully breaking a computation into methods and carefully choosing their names communicates more about your intentions to a reader than any other programming decision, besides class naming.

Methods are the granularity of overriding. A well factored superclass can always be specialized by overriding a single method, without having to copy part of the superclass code into the subclass.

Methods don't come for free. Managing all those bits and pieces of code—writing them in the first place, naming them, remembering, rediscovering, and communicating how they all fit together—all take time. If there is no benefit to be gained, bigger methods would be better than small because of the reduced management overhead.

Methods cost in performance as well. Each method invocation takes precious computer cycles. The trick to getting good performance is using methods as a lever to make your performance measurement and tuning more effective. In my experience, better factored code, with lots of small methods, both allows more accurate and concise performance measurement (because there aren't little snippets of code duplicated all over) and provides leverage for tuning (through techniques like Caching Instance Variable).

Overall, the goal of breaking your program into methods is to communicate your intent clearly with your reader, provide for future flexibility, and set yourself up for effective performance tuning where necessary.

Composed Method

You are implementing a method named with an Intention Revealing Selector (p. 49).

- How do you divide a program into methods?

Programs need to do more than just instruct a computer, they need to communicate to people as well. How your program is broken into methods (as well as how big those methods are) is one of the most important decisions you will make as you refine your code so that it communicates as clearly as possible. The decision is complicated by the many factors affecting it and the history of programming practice that has traditionally optimized machine resources at the cost of people's time.

Messages take time. The more small methods you create, the more messages you will execute. If all you were worried about was how fast your program would run, you would arrange all of your code in a single method. This radical approach to performance tuning invokes enormous human costs and ignores the realities of performance tuning well-structured code, which often results in several order-of-magnitude improvements.

Simple minded performance tuning is not the only factor suggesting that large methods are best. Following the flow of control in programs with many small methods can be difficult. Novice Smalltalk programmers often complain that they can't figure out where any "real" work is getting done. As you gain experience, you will need to understand the flow of control through several objects less often. Well chosen message names let you correctly assume the meaning of invoked code.

The opportunity to communicate through intention revealing message names is the most compelling reason to keep methods small. People can read your programs much more quickly and accurately if they can understand them in detail, then chunk those details into higher level structures. Dividing a program into methods gives you an opportunity to guide that chunking. It is a way for you to subtly communicate the structure of your system.

Small methods ease maintenance. They let you isolate assumptions. Code that has been written with the right small methods requires the change of only a few methods to correct or enhance its operation. This is true whether you are fixing bugs, adding features, or tuning performance.

Small methods also make inheritance work smoothly. If you decide to specialize the behavior of a class written with large methods, you will often find yourself copying the code from the superclass into the subclass and changing a few lines. You have introduced a multiple update problem between the superclass method and the subclass method. With small methods, overriding behavior is always a case of overriding a single method.

- *Divide your program into methods that perform one identifiable task. Keep all of the operations in a method at the same level of abstraction. This will naturally result in programs with many small methods, each a few lines long.*

You can use Composed Method top-down. While you are writing a method, you can (without having an implementation yet) invoke several smaller methods. Composed Method becomes a thought tool for breaking your development into pieces. Here is an example of a top-down Composed Method:

```
Controller>>controlActivity
    self controlInitialize.
    self controlLoop.
    self controlTerminate
```

You can also use Composed Method bottom-up, to factor common code in a single place. If you find yourself using the same expression (which might be only 3 or 2 or even 1 line of code), you can improve your code by putting the expression in its own method and invoking it as needed.

Perhaps most importantly, you can use Composed Method to discover new responsibilities while you are implementing. Any time you are sending two or more messages from one object to another in a single method, you may be able to create a Composed Method in the receiver that combines those messages. Such methods are invariably useful from other parts of your system.

FORWARD

Create objects with a Constructor Method (p. 23). Put boolean expressions into a Query Method (p. 30). Invoke Messages to get work done elsewhere, sometimes by Delegation (p. 64). Use a Temporary Variable (p. 103) for temporary storage. Represent constants with a Constant Method (p. 87).

Constructor Method

A Composed Method (p. 21) has had to create an object.

● How do you represent instance creation?

The most flexible way to represent instance creation is by a simple "new" method, followed by a series of messages from the client to the new instance. That way, if there are different combinations of parameters that make sense, the client can take advantage of just those parameters it needs.

Creating a Point in this style looks like this:

```
Point new x: 0; y: 0
```

Further flexibility is provided in this approach to half-way construct an object in one place, and then pass it off to another to finish construction. This can simplify communications if you don't have to modify the design to put all the creation parameters in one place.

On the other hand, what is the first thing you want to know about a class, once you've decided it may do what you want it to do? The first question is "What does it take to create an instance?" As a class provider, you'd like the answer to this question to be as simple as possible. With the style described above, you have to track down references to the class and read the code before you get an inkling of how to create a useable instance. If the code is complex, it may take a while before you figure out what is required and what is optional in creating an instance.

The alternative is to make sure that there is a method to represent each valid way to create an instance. Does this result in a proliferation of instance creation methods? Almost never. Most classes only have a single way to create an instance. Almost all of the exceptions only have a handful of variations. For the rare case where there really are hundreds or thousands of possible correct combinations of parameters, use Constructor Methods for the common cases and provide Accessor Methods for the remainder.

With this style of instance creation, the question "How can I create a valid instance?" can be simply answered by looking at the "instance creation" protocol of the class methods. The Intention Revealing Selectors communicate what the instance will do for you, while the Type Suggesting Parameter Names communicate the parameters required.

- *Provide methods that create well-formed instances. Pass all required parameters to them.*

Point class>>x:y: is a Constructor Method because it takes both of the required numbers as parameters.

Some people think that the keywords in the Constructor Method have to be named the same as the instance variables that will eventually be initialized while constructing an instance. You should always look for a way of expressing more intention with a selector (Intention Revealing Selector). For example, Point class>>r:theta: is a Constructor Method I add when I am working in polar coordinates:

```
Point class>>r: radiusNumber theta: thetaNumber
    ^self
            x: radiusNumber * thetaNumber cos
            y: radiusNumber * thetaNumber sin
```

SortedCollection class>>sortBlock: aBlock is a Constructor Method because it returns a SortedCollection that is ready to use. SortedCollection class>>new is also a Constructor Method because it returns a SortedCollection that is ready to use, too. It just has a default sort block.

Put Constructor Methods into a method protocol called "instance creation."

FORWARD

If the method takes parameters, you will need a Constructor Parameter Method (p. 25). Give your method an Intention Revealing Selector (p. 49) that describes the roles of the parameters, not their type. A Constructor Method that is used extensively may deserve a Shortcut Constructor Method (p. 26).

Constructor Parameter Method

BACK

A Constructor Method (p. 23) needs to pass parameters on to the new instance. You need to initialize Common State (p. 80).

- How do you set instance variables from the parameters to a Constructor Method?

Once you have the parameters of a Constructor Method to the class, how do you get them to the newly created instance?

The most flexible and consistent method is to use Setting Methods to set all the variables. Thus, a Point would be initialized with two messages:

```
Point class>>x: xNumber y: yNumber
    ^self new
        x: xNumber;
        y: yNumber;
        yourself
```

The problem I have run into with this approach is that Setting Methods can become complex. I have had to add special logic to the Setting Methods to check whether they are being sent during initialization; if so I just set the variable.

Remember the rule that says "Say things once and only once?" Special casing a Setting Method for use during initialization is a violation of the first part of that rule. You have two circumstances—state initialization during instance creation and state change during computation—but only one method. You have two things to say and you've only said one thing.

The Setting Method solution also has the drawback that if you want to see the types of all the variables, you have to look at the Type Suggesting Parameter Names in several methods. You'd like the reader to be able to look at your code and quickly understand the types of the Instance Variables.

- *Code a single method that sets all the variables. Preface its name with "set," then the names of the variables.*

Using this pattern, the code above becomes:

```
Point class>>x: xNumber y: yNumber
    ^self new
        setX: xNumber
        y: yNumber
Point>>setX: xNumber y: yNumber
    x := xNumber.
    y := yNumber.
    ^self
```

Note the Interesting Return Value in setX:y:. It is there because the return value of the method will be used as the return value of the caller.

Put Constructor Parameters Methods in a method protocol called "private."

If you are using Explicit Initialization (p. 83), now is a good time to invoke it, to communicate that initialization is part of instance creation.

Shortcut Constructor Method

You have identified a pervasive Constructor Method (p. 23).

- What is the external interface for creating a new object when a Constructor Method is too wordy?

The typical way you create a new object is to send a message to the class that creates a new instance for you; "Point x: width y: height". This is good because it is very explicit about what object is being created. If you want to find out what happens as a result of this expression, you know just where to look.

There are two problems with this style of interface for object creation. The most important is that it is wordy. If Point class>>x:y: were the only interface for creating points, I dare say the Smalltalk source file would grow by a few percent. For very commonly used objects, you can create a more concise interface by sending a message to one of the arguments that then turns around and sends the longer form.

The second problem with an explicit class-based interface for object creation is that it can be misleading. There are times when differences in the classes of the arguments change the concrete class returned by the message. For example, different kinds of Collections might need different kinds of Streams.

The very conciseness of representing object creation as a message to one of the arguments is also its weakness. Such a message can easily be mistaken for built in language syntax ("@" is the classic example). It puts a burden on the programmer to remember the message. It cannot be easily looked up by looking at the instance creation methods of the class. However, the clarity or concision gains for a constructor method can be substantial.

- *Represent object creation as a message to one of the arguments to the Constructor Method. Add no more than three of these Shortcut Constructor Methods per system you develop.*

The classic example in Smalltalk is Point creation. The Constructor Method is:

```
Point class>>x: xNumber y: yNumber
    ^self new
        setX: xNumber
        y: yNumber
```

The Shortcut Constructor Method is:

```
Number>>@ aNumber
    ^Point
        x: self
        y: aNumber
```

Interestingly, the ParcPlace image has been moving away from using Point>>extent: and Point>>corner: as Shortcut Constructor Methods for Rectangles.

Put Shortcut Constructor Methods in a method protocol called "converting."

Conversion

- How do you convert information from one object's format to another's?

Different clients may need the same information presented with different protocol. For example, one object may need to look at a Collection sorted, another with duplicates removed.

The simplest solution is to add all of the possible protocol needed to every object that may be asked of it. This might result in unnecessarily large public protocols with the resulting difficulty in publication and understanding. The same selector might need to mean different things to different clients, making this approach simply unworkable.

- *Convert from one object to another rather than overwhelm any one object's protocol.*

Some conversions are between similar objects, like changing a String of 8-bit ASCII characters to a String of 16-bit ISO characters. Some conversions are between different objects, like changing a String to a Date or a Number to a Pointer.

Conversions that return objects with similar responsibilities should use a Converter Method (p. 28). To convert to an object with different protocol use a Converter Constructor Method (p. 29).

Converter Method

You are implementing a Conversion.

- How do you represent simple conversion of an object to another object with the same protocol but different format?

For a long time, it bothered me that there was a String>>asDate method. I couldn't quite put my finger on what it was that bothered me about it, though. Then, I walked into a project where they had taken the idea of conversion to extremes. Every domain object had twenty or thirty different conversion methods. Every time a new object was added, it had to have all twenty or thirty methods before it would start working with the rest of the system.

One problem with representing conversion as methods in the object to be converted is that there is no limit to the number of methods that can be added. The protocol grows and grows without limit. Another is that it ties the receiver, however tenuously, with a class of which it would otherwise be oblivious.

I avoid the protocol explosion problem by only representing conversions with a message to the object to be converted when:

- The source and destination of conversion share the same protocol.
- There is only one reasonable way to implement the conversion.

- *Provide a method in the object to be converted that converts to the new object. Name the method by prepending "as" to the class of the object returned.*

Here are some examples. Notice that the object returned has the same protocol as the receiver (Sets act like Collections, Floats act like Numbers).

```
Collection>>asSet
Number>>asFloat
```

Put Converter Methods in a method protocol called "private."

Choose an Intention Revealing Selector (p. 49) for your conversion.

Converter Constructor Method

You need to implement Conversion (p. 28) to a new kind of object.

- How do you represent the conversion of an object to another with different protocol?

In many ways, the simplest way to communicate the presence of a conversion is a Converter Method. If I am explaining Date to you and you already know about Strings, it is tempting to say, "You can just convert a String to a Date by sending asDate to the String."

This solution risks cluttering common sources of conversion like Strings and Numbers with protocol that is irrelevant to their primary mission. The Visual Smalltalk implementation of String has 36 as... methods, half of which return objects with completely different protocols. I have seen applications where String has been "enhanced" with more than 100 Conversion Methods.

- *Make a Constructor Method that takes the object to be converted as an argument.*

For example, Date class>>fromString: is a Converter Constructor Method. It takes the String to be converted as an argument and returns a Date.

Put Converter Constructor Methods in a protocol called "instance creation."

You need to choose an Intention Revealing Selector (p. 49) for the method.

Query Method

A Composed Method (p. 21) has had to execute a boolean expression.

- How do you represent testing a property of an object?

There are actually two decisions here. The first is deciding what to return from a method that tests a property. The second is what you should name the method.

Designing the protocol for a Query Method provides you with two alternatives. The first is to return one of two objects. For example, if you have a switch that can be either on or off, you could return either #on or #off.

```
Switch>>makeOn
        status := #on
Switch>>makeOff
        status := #off
Switch>>status
        ^status
```

That leaves clients needing to know how Switch stores its status:

```
WallPlate>>update
    self switch status = #on ifTrue: [self light makeOn].
    self switch status = #off ifTrue: [self light makeOff]
```

A maintenance programmer who innocently decides to change the Symbols to #On and #Off will break the client.

It is far easier to maintain a relationship based solely on messages. Rather than status returning a Symbol, it is better for Switch to provide a single method that returns a Boolean; true if the Switch is on and false if the Switch is off.

Whether this is represented in the Switch as a variable holding a Boolean or a variable holding one of two Symbols is irrelevant to designing the protocol.

The naming question is a bit more sticky. The simplest name for a method that tests a property and returns a Boolean is just a simple name. In the example above, I'd be tempted to call the method "on":

```
Switch>>on
    "Return true if the receiver is on, otherwise return false."
```

However, this leads to confusion. Does "on" mean "is it on?" or "make it on?"

- *Provide a method that returns a Boolean. Name it by prefacing the property name with a form of "be"—is, was, will, etc.*

Here are some examples from Smalltalk:

```
isNil
isControlWanted
isEmpty
```

If you use the logical inverse of a Query Method a lot, also provide an inverse method, like notNil or notEmpty. Actually, if you can find a positive way of saying the inverse, that's even better. On the other hand, isUseful and isFull don't make much sense.

Put Query Methods in a protocol called "testing."

Comparing Method

- How do you order objects with respect to each other?

The comparison messages <, <=, >, >= are implemented mostly in Magnitude and its subclasses. They are used for all sorts of purposes—sorting, filtering, and checking for thresholds.

When you create new objects, you have the option of implementing comparison methods yourself. When I was a year or two into Smalltalk, I seem to remember implementing comparison methods any time I put a kind of object into a SortedCollection. As time went on, I used the sort block (see SortedCollection) more and more and implemented "<=" less and less.

I still implement "<=" when there is one overwhelming way to order a new object. That way, those using it can take a collection containing those objects and sort them just by saying "asSortedCollection."

Most uses of sorting in the user interface require more flexibility than can be provided by a single comparison order. Expect to use sort blocks with Temporarily Sorted Collection.

- *Implement "<=" to return true if the receiver should be ordered before the argument.*

Numbers are the obvious example of Comparing Methods. Characters and Strings also implement Comparing Methods.

If you had a Collection of timed Events, the Comparing Method could order them by time:

```
Event>><= anEvent
    ^self timestamp <= anEvent timestamp
```

Put Comparing Methods in a protocol called "comparing."

FORWARD

BACK

Ordering is often done in terms of Simple Delegation (p. 65) to the ordering of other objects. For multiple orderings, use a Temporarily Sorted Collection (p. 155).

Reversing Method

A Composed Method (p. 21) may not read right because messages are going to too many receivers. You may have a Cascade (p. 183) that doesn't look quite right because several different objects need to receive messages.

- How do you code a smooth flow of messages?

Good code has a rhythm that makes it easy to understand. Code that breaks the rhythm is harder to read and understand.

```
Point>>printOn: aStream
    x printOn: aStream.
    aStream nextPutAll: ' @ '.
    y printOn: aStream
```

Here we have messages going to three different objects. We want to read this as a three part operation, but because the operations are on three different objects it is hard to put the pieces together.

We can solve the problem by making sure that all messages go through a single object. However, creating new selectors just for the fun of it is a bad idea. Each selector in the system must justify its existence by solving a real problem; encoding an important decision.

Adding a new method with a new selector to make code read more smoothly is a good use of the selector namespace.

- *Code a method on the parameter. Derive its name from the original message. Take the original receiver as a parameter to the new method. Implement the method by sending the original message to the original receiver.*

By defining Stream>>print:, we can smooth out the above method:

```
Stream>>print: anObject
        anObject printOn: self
Point>>printOn: aStream
        aStream
            print: x;
            nextPutAll: ' @ ';
            print: y
```

This pattern seems to veer perilously close to the realm of pure aesthetics. However, I often find that the desire to use it is followed closely by the absolute need to use it. As soon as you have all the messages going to a single object, that object can easily vary without affecting any of the parameters.

Put Reversing Methods in a method protocol named after the message being reversed. For example, Stream>>print: is in the method protocol "printing."

Method Object

BACK

You have a method that does not simplify well with Composed Method (p. 21).

- How do you code a method where many lines of code share many arguments and temporary variables?

The behavior at the center of a complex system is often complicated. That complexity is generally not recognized at first, so the behavior is represented as a single method. Gradually that method grows and grows, gaining more lines, more parameters, and more temporary variables, until it is a monstrous mess.

Far from improving communications, applying Composed Method to such a method only obscures the situation. Since all the parts of such a method generally need all the temporary variables and parameters, any piece of the method you break off requires six or eight parameters.

The solution is to create an object to represent an invocation of the method and use the shared namespace of instance variables in the object to enable further simplification using Composed Method. However, these objects have a very different flavor than most objects. Most objects are nouns, these are verbs. Most objects are easily explainable to clients, these are not because they have no analog in the real world. However, Method Objects are worth their strange nature. Because they represent such an important part of the behavior of the system, they often end up at the center of the architecture.

- *Create a class named after the method. Give it an instance variable for the receiver of the original method, each argument, and each temporary variable. Give it a Constructor Method that takes the original receiver and the method arguments. Give it one instance method, #compute, implemented by copying the body of the original method. Replace the method with one that creates an instance of the new class and sends it #compute.*

This is the last pattern I added to this book. I wasn't going to include it because I use it so seldom. Then it convinced an important client to give me a big contract. I realized that when you need it, you REALLY need it.

The code looked like this:

```
Obligation>>sendTask: aTask job: aJob
    | notProcessed processed copied executed |
    ...150 lines of heavily commented code...
```

First, I tried Composed Method. Every time I tried to break off a piece of the method, I realized I would have to send it both parameters and all four temps:

```
Obligation>>prepareTask: aTask job: aJob notProcessed:
notProcessedCollection processed: processedCollection
copied: copiedCollection executed: executedCollection
```

Not only was this ugly, but the resulting invocation didn't save any lines of code (see Indented Control Flow, below). After fifteen minutes or so of struggle, I went back to the original method and used Method Object. First I created the class:

```
Class: TaskSender
    superclass: Object
    instance variables: obligation task job notProcessed
processed copied executed
```

Notice that the name of the class is taken directly from the selector of the original method. Notice also that the original receiver, both arguments, and all four temps became instance variables.

The Constructor Method took the original receiver and both arguments as parameters:

```
TaskSender class>>obligation: anObligation task: aTask
job: aJob
    ^self new
        setObligation: anObligation
        task: aTask
        job: aJob
```

Next I copied the code from the original method. The only change I made was textually replacing "aTask" with "task" and "aJob" with "job," since parameters are named differently than instance variables. Oh, I also deleted the declaration of the temps, since they were now instance variables.

```
TaskSender>>compute
    ...150 lines of heavily commented code...
```

Then I changed the original method to create and invoke a TaskSender:

```
Obligation>>sendTask: aTask job: aJob
    (TaskSender
        obligation: self
        task: aTask
        job: aJob) compute
```

I tried out the method to make sure I hadn't broken anything. Since all I had been doing was moving text around, and I did it carefully, the revised method and its associated object worked the first time.

Now came the fun part. Since all the pieces of the method now shared the same instance variables, I could use Composed Method without having to pass any parameters. For example, the piece of code that prepared a Task became a method called #prepareTask.

The whole job took about two hours, but by the time I was done the #compute method read like documentation; I had eliminated three of the instance variables, the code as a whole was half of its original length, and I'd found and fixed a bug in the original code.

Execute Around Method

- How do you represent pairs of actions that have to be taken together?

It is common for two messages to an object to have to be invoked in tandem. When a file is opened, it has to be closed. When a context is pushed, it has to be popped.

The obvious way to represent this is by publishing both methods as part of the external protocol of the object. Clients need to explicitly invoke both, in the right order, and make sure that if the first is called, the second is called as well. This makes learning and using the object more difficult and leads to many defects, such as file descriptor leaks.

- *Code a method that takes a Block as an argument. Name the method by appending "During: aBlock" to the name of the first method that needs to be invoked. In the body of the Execute Around Method, invoke the first method, evaluate the block, then invoke the second method.*

I learned this pattern from Cursor>>showWhile:

```
Cursor>>showWhile: aBlock
    | old |
    old := Cursor currentCursor.
    self show.
    aBlock value.
    old show
```

I use it lots of places. For example, I use it for making sure files get closed.

```
File>>openDuring: aBlock
    self open.
    aBlock value.
    self close
```

You will often want to wrap the Block evaluation in an exception handler so you are assured the second message gets sent.

```
File>>openDuring: aBlock
    self open.
    [aBlock value] ensure: [self close]
```

Put Execute Around Methods in a method protocol named after the operations they encapsulate. For example, File>>openDuring: goes in the method protocol "opening."

You need to give your method an Intention Revealing Selector (p. 49).

Debug Printing Method

● How do you code the default printing method?

Smalltalk provides a single mechanism for turning objects into printable strings; printOn:. Strings are great because they fit nicely into generic interface components; lists display strings; tables display strings; text editors and input fields display strings.

Strings are also useful in generic programming tools, like the Inspector. As a programmer, you can often look at the string generated by an object and instantly diagnose a problem.

The two audiences for strings generated by objects, you and your client, are often in conflict. You want all the internal, structural details of your object laid out in one place so you don't have to go searching layers and layers of objects to find what you want. Your client assumes the object is working correctly and just wants to see externally relevant aspects of the object in the string.

VisualWorks has taken the valuable step of separating these two uses of object-to-string conversion. If you want a client-consumable string, you send "displayString." If you want a programmer-consumable string, you send "printString." For Smalltalks with a single message for printing, you need to choose which audience you will address.

● *Override printOn: to provide information about an object's structure to the programmer.*

Associations print so that programmers can read them:

```
Association>> printOn: aStream
    aStream
        print: self key;
        nextPutAll: '->';
        print: self value
```

The saving grace of this pattern is that all the user interface builders have ways of parameterizing which message they will send to objects to get strings. Thus, when you create a list and send it some objects, you can also say "...and send the message 'userString' to the objects to get strings."

Put Printing Methods in the method protocol "printing."

Method Comment

You have written a Composed Method (p. 21).

- How do you comment methods?

Back in the days of assembly language programming, the distance between what you intended as a programmer and how the computer forced you to express that intention was enormous. Every few lines (sometimes on every line), you needed a little story to help you understand what the next few instructions really meant.

As programming languages progressed, moving the expression closer to what it really meant, the habit of commenting every few lines relaxed somewhat. Many commenting standards settled on a comment at the beginning of a procedure, explaining the purpose of the procedure and describing the arguments and return value.

I find no value in this kind of "template" comment. Someone recently asked me point blank, "What percentage of your methods have comments?" I answered, "Between 0 and 1 percent." Oh the uproar! As a sanity check, I asked a developer at one of my clients (where I had taught Smalltalk based on an earlier version of these patterns) what percentage of the methods of their 200 class system had comments. His answer, "between 0 and 1 percent." "Has that ever been a problem?" "No, never."

I have certainly heard extravagant claims of "self documenting" code over the years. Shoot, Forth was supposed to be self documenting. What is it about Smalltalk code written with these patterns that lets it communicate tactical information without any supporting prose?

The information in the "template" comment is captured in the code with various patterns; Intention Revealing Selector communicates what the method does; Type Suggesting Parameter Name says what the arguments are expected to be; and various types of method patterns suggest return types, like Query Method for methods returning Booleans.

There is another important topic to communicate about a procedure—how it handles the various cases it is coded for. In Smalltalk, important cases become objects in their own right (see Choosing Message below), so each method only computes a single case. The result is code that communicates all the necessary tactical information to the reader.

Regardless of how well the system as a whole is put together, the big picture cannot easily be read method by method. There has to be another way of teaching the reader about the system as a whole. I use literate programs, although class and package comments will do in a pinch. However, trying to shoehorn a description of the architecture into a method comment is unlikely to work well, if only because the reader most likely won't stumble across it.

- *Communicate important information that is not obvious from the code in a comment at the beginning of the method.*

Here are examples of information that can be difficult to communicate solely through the code:

- Method dependencies—Sometimes one method must be invoked before another can execute correctly. A comment can warn the reader not to invoke one without the other. Sometimes you can use Composed Method or Execute Around Method to communicate the same information.

- To-do—I often write comments while I am prototyping to remind myself of some thought I don't want to lose. "Look at using a Dictionary later for efficiency," for example. When I reconsider the thought later, I delete the comment after choosing whether to follow it.

- Reasons for change, particularly base class—If you need to change something, the reason for the change is often not immediately apparent in the code. This often occurs when changing a method supplied by a Smalltalk vendor. A comment helps a reader understand why you did what you did if you can't make the code say it.

Here is my favorite example of a useless comment:

```
(self flags bitAnd: 2r1000) = 1 "Am I visible?"
    ifTrue: [...]
```

A quick look at Composed Method yields:

```
isVisible
    ^(self flags bitAnd: 2r1000) = 1
```

And the original code turns into:

```
self isVisible
    ifTrue: [...]
```

I expect you to be skeptical of this pattern. Here's an experiment you can perform in the privacy of your own workstation. Write code with comments for every method. Go through your methods one by one and delete only those comments that duplicate exactly what the code says. If you can't delete a comment, see if you can refactor the code using these patterns (Composed Method and Intention Revealing Selector are especially useful) to communicate the same thing. I will be willing to bet that when you are done you will have almost no comments left.

One last example from client code:

```
Bin>>run
    "Tell my station to process me."
    self station process: self
```

You can translate the code directly into the comment:

English	Code
Tell my station	self station
to process	process:
me	self

Messages

Messages are the heartbeat of a Smalltalk program. Without messages, there would be no program. Deftly managing this heartbeat is the first skill of the expert Smalltalk programmer. When you learn to see your program in terms of patterns of messages and you learn what can be done to that stream of messages to solve problems, then you will be able to solve any problem you can imagine in Smalltalk.

Procedural languages explicitly make choices. When you code up a case statement, you say once and for all what all the possibilities are. In Smalltalk, you use messages to make choices for you. The extra added bonus is that the set of choices is not set in concrete. You can come along later and add new choices without affecting the existing choices just by defining a new class.

This section talks about the tactical ways you can use the message stream. It gives you a toolbox of techniques for solving problems by manipulating the communication between objects.

Message

A Composed Method (p. 21) needs work done.

- How do you invoke computation?

In the earliest days of computing, this wasn't even a question. A program was one big routine that executed from start to finish.

As soon as programs got at all complicated, "program-as-a-routine" broke down. Conceptually, it was just too hard to manipulate the whole program at once. The limited resources of the era also came into play. When you had the same code duplicated in many places, you could save space by using a single copy of the code and invoking it everywhere you needed. The two factors, mental overload and memory overload, worked with each other. By giving the broken-out parts of the routine names, you saved space and you got a convenient tool for understanding the program a piece at a time.

Here things stood for a number of years. The client would invoke a subroutine. The subroutine would run. The client would regain control.

At the same time, there was a growing realization that a disciplined use of control structures was critical to the quality and cost of a program. If-then-else and case statements were invented to capture common ways to vary the execution of a program.

Simula brilliantly combined these two ideas. Conditional code says "execute this part of the routine or that part." A subroutine call says "execute that code over there." A message says "execute this routine over here or that routine over there, I don't really care."

Smalltalk went a step further by making messages the sole control structure in the system. All procedural control structures, conditionals and loops, are implemented in terms of messages. For the most part, explicit conditional logic plays a much smaller role in a Smalltalk program than a procedural program. Messages do most of the work.

- *Send a named message and let the receiving object decide what to do with it.*

Since everything in Smalltalk happens as a result of a message, it's tough to pick out one or two examples. #size is a message you can send to any object to get the number of elements (exclusive of named variables) it contains.

Use Delegation (p. 64) to get another object to do work for you. A Choosing Message (p. 45) invokes one of several alternatives. A Decomposing Message (p. 47) documents intent and provides for later refinement. An Intention Revealing Message (p. 48) maps intention to implementation. Use Super (p. 59) to invoke behavior in a superclass.

Choosing Message

You are using a Message (p. 43).

- How do you execute one of several alternatives?

The long term health of a system is all about managing themes and variations. When you first write a program, you have a particular theme in mind. Setting the program free in the world inevitably suggests all sorts of variations on what you first thought was a simple task.

Procedural programs implement variations with conditional logic, either if-then-else or case statements. Two problems arise from such hard-coded logic. First, you cannot add a new variation without modifying the logic. This can be a ticklish operation, getting the new variation in without disturbing the existing variations. Second, such logic tends to propagate. You do not have to account for the variation in one place, you have to account for it in several. Adding a new variation means tickling all of the places where the logic lives.

Messages provide a disciplined way to handle theme-and-variation programming. Because the variations live in different objects, they have much less opportunity to interfere with each other than just putting the variations in different parts of the same routine. The client, the object invoking the variations, is also isolated from what variation is currently active.

Adding a new variation is as simple as adding a new object that provides the same set of messages the other variations provide and introducing it to the object that wants to invoke the variations.

Sometimes, even when beginners have several kinds of objects, they still resort to conditional logic:

```
responsible := (anEntry isKindOf: Film)
    ifTrue: [anEntry producer]
    ifFalse: [anEntry author]
```

Code like this can always be transformed into communicative, flexible code by using a Choosing Message:

```
Film>>responsible
    ^self producer
Entry>>responsible
    ^self author
```

Now you can write:

```
responsible := anEntry responsible
```

But you probably don't need the Explaining Temporary Variable any more.

- *Send a message to one of several different kinds of objects, each of which executes one alternative.*

When you begin a program, you won't be able to anticipate the variations. As your program matures, you will see explicit conditional logic creep in. When you can see the same logic repeated in several places, it is time to find a way to represent the alternatives as objects and invoke them with a choosing message.

Here are some examples of choosing messages:

Message	Alternatives
Number>>+ aNumber	Different code will be invoked depending on what kind of Number the receiver is. Floats add differently than Integers, which add differently than Fractions.
Object>>printOn: aStream	Every object has the opportunity to change how it is represented to the programmer as a String.
Collection>>includes:	Different collections implement this very differently. The default implementation takes time proportional to the size of the collection. Others take constant time.

If a Choosing Message is sent to self, it is done so in anticipation of future refinement by inheritance.

Give the message an Intention Revealing Selector (p. 49). Look at the section on Methods (p. 20) for examples of the kind of code that can be invoked as variations.

Decomposing Message

You are using a Message (p. 43) to break a computation into parts.

- How do you invoke parts of a computation?

A Choosing Message gets work done. It is the equivalent of a case statement in procedural languages. Depending on the circumstance, different code is invoked.

Another way messages are used is to break a computation down into pieces. As you are writing the code, you don't think about possible variations. A method is getting too big and you need to break it into parts so you can understand it better. Alternatively, you may have noticed that two or more methods have similar parts and you'd like to put the parts in a single method.

This is very similar to the way subroutines are used in procedural programming. You take a big routine and break it into pieces.

Smalltalk code reveals a much more aggressive attitude towards decomposing code than other languages. Most style guides say, "Keep the code for a routine on one page." Most good Smalltalk methods fit into a few lines, certainly less than ten and often three or four.

Partly this is possible because the abstractions Smalltalk provides are higher level than what you find in most languages. You don't spend three or four lines expressing iteration, you spend one word. Partly, it is possible because Smalltalk's programming tools let you manage smaller pieces easily.

- *Send several messages to "self."*

The classic example of this from the original Smalltalk image was:

```
Controller>>controlActivity
    self
        controlInitialize;
        controlLoop;
        controlTerminate
```

Later, these messages all became Choosing Messages because they were all overridden a hundred different ways.

Use Composed Method (p. 21) to break the method into pieces. Give each method an Intention Revealing Selector (p. 49). Use Intention Revealing Messages (p. 48) to communicate intent separate from implementation.

Intention Revealing Message

You are using a Message (p. 43) to invoke a computation. You may be hiding the use of Pluggable Behavior (p. 69).

- How do you communicate your intent when the implementation is simple?

These messages have to be the most frustrating part of learning Smalltalk. You see a message like "highlight:" and you think, "This has to be something interesting." Instead, you see:

```
ParagraphEditor>>highlight: aRectangle
    self reverse: aRectangle
```

What's going on?

Communication. Most importantly, one line methods are there to communicate. If I have the above method, the rest of the code in the object can be written in terms of highlighting. I want to highlight an area, so I send highlight. Makes sense.

I could mechanically replace all the invocations of highlight with invocations of reverse. The code would run the same. However, all the invoking code reveals the implementation—"I highlight by reversing a Rectangle."

The other advantage of code written to reveal intention and conceal implementation is that it is much easier to refine by inheritance. If I want a ParagraphEditor that highlights in color, I can make a subclass of ParagraphEditor and override a single method—highlight:.

Intention Revealing Messages are the most extreme case of writing for readers instead of the computer. As far as the computer is concerned, both versions are fine. The one that separates intention (what you want done) from implementation (how it is done) communicates better to a person.

- *Send a message to "self." Name the message so it communicates what is to be done rather than how it is to be done. Code a simple method for the message.*

Here are some examples of Intention Revealing Messages and their implementation:

```
Collection>>isEmpty
    ^self size = 0
Number>>reciprocal
    ^1 / self
Object>>= anObject
    ^self == anObject
```

FORWARD

Give the message an Intention Revealing Selector (p. 49).

Intention Revealing Selector

BACK

You may be naming a method: a Constructor Method (p. 23), Conversion Method (p. 28), Converter Constructor Method (p. 26), or Execute Around Method (p. 37). You may be naming a message: Decomposing Message (p. 47), Choosing Message (p. 45), or Intention Revealing Message (p. 48). You may be implementing Double Dispatch (p. 55).

- What do you name a method?

You have two options in naming methods. The first is to name the method after how it accomplishes its task. Thus, searching methods would be called:

```
Array>>linearSearchFor:
Set>>hashedSearchFor:
BTree>>treeSearchFor:
```

The most important argument against this style of naming is that it doesn't communicate well. If I have code that invokes three other objects, I have to read and understand three different pieces of implementation before I can understand the code.

Also, naming methods this way results in code that knows what kind of object it is dealing with. If I have code that works with an Array, I can't substitute a BTree or a Set.

The second option is to name a method after what it is supposed to accomplish and leave "how" to the various method bodies. This is hard work, especially when you only have a single implementation. Your mind is filled with how you are about to accomplish the task, so it's natural that the name follow "how." The effort of moving the names of method from "how" to "what" is worth it, both long term and short term. The resulting code will be easier to read and more flexible.

- *Name methods after what they accomplish.*

Applying this to the example above, we would name all of the messages "searchFor:."

```
Collection>>searchFor:
```

Really, though, searching is a way of implementing a more general concept, inclusion. Trying to name the message after this more general "what" leads us to "includes:" as a selector.

Collection>>includes:

Here's a simple exercise that will help you generalize names of messages with a single implementation. Imagine a second, very different implementation. Then, ask yourself if you'd give that method the same name. If so, you've probably abstracted the name as much as you know how to at the moment.

FORWARD

Once you name a method, write its body using Composed Method (p. 21). Format the selector in the method with an Inline Message Pattern (p. 172). Add a Collecting Parameter (p. 75)if necessary to collect results.

Dispatched Interpretation

- How can two objects cooperate when one wishes to conceal its representation?

Encoding is inevitable in programming. At some point you say, "Here is some information. How am I going to represent it?" This decision to encode information happens a hundred times a day.

Back in the days when data was separated from computation, and seldom the twain should meet, encoding decisions were critical. Any encoding decision you made was propagated to many different parts of the computation. If you got the encoding wrong, the cost of change was enormous. The longer it took to find the mistake, the more ridiculous the bill.

Objects change all this. How you distribute responsibility among objects is the critical decision, encoding is a distant second. For the most part, in well factored programs, only a single object is interested in a piece of information. That object directly references the information and privately performs all the needed encoding and decoding.

Sometimes, however, information in one object must influence the behavior of another. When the uses of the information are simple, or the possible choices based on the information limited, it is sufficient to send a message to the encoded object. Thus, the fact that boolean values are represented as instances of one of two classes, True and False, is hidden behind the message #ifTrue:ifFalse:.

```
True>>ifTrue: trueBlock ifFalse: falseBlock
    ^trueBlock value
False>>ifTrue: trueBlock ifFalse: falseBlock
    ^falseBlock value
```

We could encode boolean values some other way, and as long as we provided the same protocol, no client would be the wiser.

Sets interact with their elements like this. Regardless of how an object is represented, as long it can respond to #= and #hash, it can be put in a Set.

Sometimes, encoding decisions can be hidden behind intermediate objects. An ASCII String encoded as eight-bit bytes hides that fact by conversing with the outside world in terms of Characters:

```
String>>at: anInteger
    ^Character asciiValue: (self basicAt: anInteger)
```

When there are many different types of information to be encoded, and the behavior of clients changes based on the information, these simple strategies won't work. The problem is that you don't want each of a hundred clients to explicitly record in a case statement what all the types of information are.

For example, consider a graphical Shape represented by a sequence of line, curve, stroke, and fill commands. Regardless of how the Shape is represented internally, it can provide a message #commandAt: anInteger that returns a Symbol representing the command and #argumentsAt: anInteger that returns an array of arguments. We could use these messages to write a PostScriptShapePrinter that would convert a Shape to PostScript:

```
PostScriptShapePrinter>>display: aShape
    1 to: aShape size do:
        [:each || command arguments |
        command := aShape commandAt: each.
        arguments := aShape argumentsAt: each.
        command = #line ifTrue:
            [self
                printPoint: (arguments at: 1);
                space;
                printPoint: (arguments at: 2);
                space;
                nextPutAll: 'line'].
        command = #curve...
        ...]
```

Every client that wanted to make decisions based on what commands were in a Shape would have to have the same case statement, violating the "once and only once" rule. We need a solution where the case statement is hidden inside of the encoded object.

- *Have the client send a message to the encoded object. Pass a parameter to which the encoded object will send decoded messages.*

The simplest example of this is Collection>>do:. No matter what kind of collection you have, you can always send it #do:. By passing a one argument Block (or any other object that responds to #value:), you are assured that the code will work, no matter whether the Collection is encoded as a linear list, an array, a hash table, or a balanced tree.

This is a simplified case of Dispatched Interpretation because there is only a single message coming back. For the most part, there will be several messages. For example, we can use this pattern with the Shape example. Rather than have a case statement for every command, we have a method in PostScriptShapePrinter for every command. For example:

```
PostScriptShapePrinter>>lineFrom: fromPoint to: toPoint
    self
        printPoint: fromPoint;
        space;
        printPoint: toPoint;
        space;
        nextPutAll: 'line'
```

Rather than Shapes providing #commandAt: and #argumentsAt:, they provide #sendCommandAt: anInteger to: anObject, where #lineFrom:to: is one of the messages that could be sent back. Then, the original display code could read:

```
PostScriptShapePrinter>>display: aShape
    1 to: aShape size do:
        [:each |
        aShape
            sendCommandAt: each
            to: self]
```

This could be further simplified by giving Shapes the responsibility to iterate over themselves:

```
Shape>>sendCommandsTo: anObject
    1 to: self size do:
        [:each |
        self
            sendCommandAt: each
            to: anObject]
```

With this, the original display code becomes:

```
PostScriptShapePrinter>>display: aShape
    aShape sendCommandsTo: self
```

The name "dispatched interpretation" comes from the distribution of responsibility. The encoded object "dispatches" a message to the client. The client "interprets" the message. Thus, the Shape dispatches messages like #lineFrom:to: and #curveFrom:mid:to:. It's up to the clients to interpret the messages, with the PostScriptShapePrinter creating PostScript and the ShapeDisplayer displaying on the screen.

You will have to design a Mediating Protocol (p. 57) of messages to be sent back. Computations where both objects have decoding to do need Double Dispatch (p. 55).

Double Dispatch

You have a Dispatched Interpretation (p. 51) between two families of objects. You may be implementing a complex Equality Method (p. 124).

- How can you code a computation that has many cases, the cross product of two families of classes?

This pattern helps manage another of Smalltalk's engineering compromises—method dispatch. When you send a message to an object, and you include an argument, only the class of the receiver is taken into account when looking for a corresponding method. Ninety-nine percent of the time this causes you no trouble. There are a few cases, though, where the logic to be invoked really depends not just on the class of the receiver, but the class of one of the arguments as well. In fact, which object is the receiver and which is the argument may be entirely arbitrary.

		Argument	
		C	D
		---	---
Receiver	A	Method 1	Method 2
	B	Method 3	Method 4

One classic example where this relationship exists is arithmetic. When you add an Integer to an Integer you want one method, when you add a Float to a Float you want another, an Integer and a Float another, and a Float and an Integer another.

The procedural solution to this situation is to have a big case statement. Like all explicit case logic, this is difficult to maintain and extend, even though it has the advantage of putting all the program logic in one place.

The solution is adding a layer of messages that get both objects involved in the computation. As with Self Delegation, this causes you to create more messages, but the additional complexity is worth it.

- *Send a message to the argument. Append the class name of the receiver to the selector. Pass the receiver as an argument.*

The arithmetic example can be coded as follows. Integer and Float both Double Dispatch to the argument:

```
Integer>>+ aNumber
    ^aNumber addInteger: self
Float>>+ aNumber
    ^aNumber addFloat: self
```

Integer and Float both have to implement both flavors of addition. The Integer-Integer and Float-Float cases are handled as primitives.

```
Integer>>addInteger: anInteger
    <primitive: 1>
Float>>addFloat: aFloat
    <primitive: 2>
```

When you have one number of each class, you have to convert the Integer to a Float and start over:

```
Integer>>addFloat: aFloat
       ^self asFloat addFloat: aFloat
Float>>addInteger: anInteger
       ^self addFloat: anInteger asFloat
```

In the worst case, Double Dispatch can lead to N × M methods, where N is the number of classes of the original receiver and M is the number of classes of the original argument. Practically speaking, the receiver classes are usually related by inheritance, as are the argument classes, so many common implementations can be factored out.

A reviewer suggested another good use for Double Dispatch—implementing drag-and-drop operations. You want to execute different code depending on what kind of object is being dragged over what kind of receiver. The simplest and most flexible way to implemement this is with Double Dispatch.

Create a Mediating Protocol (p. 57) with which the objects communicate. Type Suggesting Parameter Names (p. 174) are important for keeping track of how much you know at any stage of the process.

Mediating Protocol

You are implementing Dispatched Interpretation (p. 51) or Double Dispatch (p. 55).

●   How do you code the interaction between two objects that need to remain independent?

For the most part, when you write a program that involves the cooperation of two objects, you create methods as needed. The dialog grows organically. When you finish, the two objects work together, but you don't necessarily have a strong sense of all the messages flowing back and forth.

Most of the time, this sort of ad hoc interaction doesn't cost you much. The changes you need to make involve changing one object or the other and occasionally adding to the messages going between them.

You need to make the protocol between the objects more visible when you decide to replace one or the other of them. The important question for you then becomes, "Exactly what messages flow between these two objects?"

When you find the answer, a list of message selectors, you will probably have some work to do. First, you need to look at the words in the selectors and see if they form a coherent system. Protocols that grow piecemeal tend to accumulate little inconsistencies. Sometimes, you will not have consistent opposites in the messages, as in #show being the opposite of #makeInvisible. Sometimes, you will not have consistently made selectors plural, as in #addEmployees: being the opposite of #removeAllEmployees:.

Because you are finding it necessary to replace one of the objects in the interaction, it is likely that others will have to create other replacements in the future. If the words in the protocol are consistent and clearly presented, they will be able to quickly create their replacements, using your code as examples.

- *Refine the protocol between the objects so the words used are consistent.*

In VisualWorks, #value and #value: is the Mediating Protocol between the user interface components and the application model.

In the Double Dispatch example, the Mediating Protocol is #addFloat: and #addInteger:. Of course, if we finished mixed mode arithmetic the protocol would be much larger.

I worked with Smalltalk/V for the Macintosh for a couple of years. One of the exercises I tried was replacing the Smalltalk-programmed TextPane with a wrapper around the native Macintosh text editor. Smalltalk/V used a Model/Pane/Dispatcher-based user interface framework, so there was a TextDispatcher associated with the pane. Its purpose was to interpret user input and pass along meaningful messages to the pane.

For a while, I tried just sticking the new pane in and debugging my way to health. It didn't take long before I realized there was no way that was going to work. There was just too much going on between the TextPane and the TextDispatcher. So I sat down with the code and recorded every message that went from the pane to the dispatcher and vice versa. In the end, I had only a handful of messages going from the pane to the dispatcher, but the dispatcher was sending the pane 56 different messages.

With this Mediating Protocol of 56 messages in place, I could sit down and design the new pane to support those messages. When I got them all implemented, I knew I was done.

Put all the methods to support a Mediating Protocol in a single method protocol, so they are easy to find and duplicate.

Examine each message to make sure it has an Intention Revealing Selector (p. 49).

Super

You are sending a Message (p. 43).

- How can you invoke superclass behavior?

An object executes in a rich context of state and behavior, created by composing together the contexts of its class and all of its class' superclasses. Most of the time, code in the class can be written as if the entire universe of methods it has available is flat. That is, take the union of all the methods up the superclass chain and that's what you have to work with.

Working this way has many advantages. It minimizes any given method's reliance on inheritance structure. If a method invokes another method on self, as long as that method is implemented somewhere in the chain, the invoking method is happy. This gives you great freedom to refactor code without having to make massive changes to methods that assume the location of some method.

There are important exceptions to this model. In particular, inheritance makes it possible to override a method in a superclass. What if the subclass method wants some aspect of the superclass method? Good style boils down to one rule: say things once and only once. If the subclass method were to contain a copy of the code from the superclass method, the result would no longer be easy to maintain. We would have to remember to update both or (potentially) many copies at once. How can we resolve the tension between the need to override, the need to retain the illusion of a flat space of methods, and the need to factor code completely?

- *Invoke code in a superclass explicitly by sending a message to "super" instead of "self." The method corresponding to the message will be found in the superclass of the class implementing the sending method.*

One example of where you want to extend superclass behavior is initialization, where not only does the state defined by the superclass need to be initialized, but also the state defined by the subclass.

Always check code using "super" carefully. Change "super" to "self" if doing so does not change how the code executes. One of the most annoying bugs I've ever tried to track down involved a use of super that didn't do anything at the time I wrote it and invoked a different selector than the one for the currently executing method. I later overrode that method in the subclass and spent half a day trying to figure out why it wasn't being invoked. My brain had overlooked the fact that the receiver was "super" instead of "self," and I proceeded on that assumption for several frustrating hours.

Extending Super (p. 60) adds behavior to the superclass. Modifying Super (p. 62) changes the superclass' behavior.

Extending Super

You are using Super (p. 59).

- How do you add to a superclass' implementation of a method?

Any use of super reduces the flexibility of the resulting code. You now have a method that assumes not just that somewhere there is an implementation of a particular method, but that the implementation has to exist in the superclass chain above the class that contains the method. This assumption is seldom a big problem, but you should be aware of the tradeoff you are making.

If you are avoiding duplication of code by using super, the tradeoff is quite reasonable. For instance, if a superclass has a method that initializes some instance variables, and your class wants to initialize the variables it has introduced, super is the right solution. Rather than have code like:

```
Class: Super
        superclass: Object
        instance variables: a

Super class>>new
        ^self basicNew initialize
Super>>initialize
        a := self defaultA
```

and rather than extending initialization in a subclass like this:

```
Class: Sub
        superclass: Super
        instance variables: b

Sub class>>new
        ^self basicNew
                initialize;
                initializeB
Sub>>initializeB
        b := self defaultB
```

using super you can implement both initializations explicitly:

```
Sub>>initialize
        super initialize.
        b := self defaultB
```

and not have Sub override "new" at all. The result is a more direct expression of the intent of the code. Make sure Supers are initialized when they are created and extend the meaning of initialization in Sub.

- *Override the method and send a message to "super" in the overriding method.*

Another example of Extending Super is display. If you have a subclass of a Figure that needs to display just like the superclass, but with a border, you could implement it like this:

```
BorderedFigure>>display
    super display.
    self displayBorder
```

Modifying Super

You are using Super (p. 59).

- How do you change part of the behavior of a superclass' method without modifying it?

This problem introduces a tighter coupling between subclass and superclass than Extending Super. Not only are we assuming that a superclass implements the method we are modifying, we are assuming that the superclass is doing something we need to change.

Often, situations like this can best be addressed by refactoring methods with Composed Method so you can use pure overriding. For example, the following initialization code could be modified by using super.

```
Class: IntegerAdder
    superclass: Object
    instance variables: sum count

IntegerAdder>>initialize
    sum := 0.
    count := 0

Class: FloatAdder
    superclass: IntegerAdder
    instance variables:

FloatAdder>>initialize
    super initialize.
    sum := 0.0
```

A better solution is to recognize that IntegerAdder>>initialize is actually doing four things: representing and assigning the default values for each of two variables. Refactoring with Composed Method yields:

```
IntegerAdder>>initialize
    sum := self defaultSum.
    count := self defaultCount
IntegerAdder>>defaultSum
    ^0
IntegerAdder>>defaultCount
    ^0

FloatAdder>>defaultSum
    ^0.0
```

However, sometimes you have to work with superclasses that are not completely factored (i.e. the superclass does not implement #defaultSum). You are faced with the choice of either copying code or using super and accepting the costs of tighter subclass/superclass coupling. Most of the time, the additional coupling will not prove to be a problem. Communicate your desired changes with the owner of the superclass. In the meantime:

- *Override the method and invoke "super," then execute the code to modify the results.*

Another example from the display realm is if you have a subclass whose color is different from the superclass'.

```
SuperFigure>>initialize
        color := Color white.
        size := 0@0
SubFigure>>initialize
        super initialize.
        color := Color beige
```

FORWARD

Again, the better solution would be to use a Default Value Method (p. 86) to represent the default color, and then override just that method.

Delegation

BACK

A Composed Method (p. 21) needs work done by another object. A Message (p. 43) invokes computation in another object.

- How does an object share implementation without inheritance?

Inheritance is the primary built-in mechanism for sharing implementation in Smalltalk. However, inheritance in Smalltalk is limited to a single superclass. What if you want to implement a new object like A but also like B? Also, inheritance carries with it potentially staggering long-term costs. Code in subclasses isn't just written in Smalltalk. It is written in the context of every variable and method in every superclass. In deep, rich hierarchies, you may have to read and understand many superclasses before you can understand even the simplest method in a subclass.

Factored Superclass explains how to make effective use of inheritance at minimal development cost. You will encounter situations where you will recognize common implementation, but where Factored Superclass is not appropriate. How can you respond?

- *Pass part of its work on to another object.*

For example, since many objects need to display, all objects in the system delegate to a brush-like object (Pen in Visual Smalltalk, GraphicsContext in VisualAge and VisualWorks) for display. That way, all the detailed display code can be concentrated in a single class and the rest of the system can have a simplified view of displaying.

Use Simple Delegation (p. 65) when the delegate need know nothing about the original object. Use Self Delegation (p. 67) when the identity of the original object or some of its state is needed by the delegate.

Simple Delegation

You need Delegation (p. 64) to a self-contained object. You may be implementing one of the following methods: Collection Accessor Method (p. 96), Equality Method (p. 124), or Hashing Method (p. 126).

- How do you invoke a disinterested delegate?

When you use delegation, there are two main issues that help clarify what flavor of delegation you need. First, is the identity of the delegating object important? This might be true if a client object passes itself along, expecting to be notified of some part of the work actually done by the delegate. The delegate doesn't want to inform the client of its existence so it needs access to the delegating object. Second, is the state of the delegating object important to the delegate? Delegates are often simple, even state-less objects, in order to be as widely useful as possible. If so, the delegate is likely to require state from the delegating object to accomplish its job.

There are many cases of delegation where the answer to these two questions is "no." The delegate has no reason to need the identity of the delegating object. The delegate is self-contained enough to accomplish its job without additional state.

- *Delegate messages unchanged.*

The typical example of this is an object that acts like a Collection (at least a little) but has lots of other protocol. Rather than waste inheritance by subclassing one of the collection classes, your object refers to a Collection. From a client's perspective, though, you respond to protocol like do: or at:put:.

The Collection doesn't care who invoked it. No state from the delegating object is required. The identity of the delegating object is irrelevant.

Here's an example—a Vector that holds only Numbers. We could implement it by subclassing Collection, but there are likely to be many messages that don't make sense for a Vector. Rather than subclass Collection and block out scads of messages, we can subclass object and delegate only those messages we want.

```
Vector
     superclass: Object
     instance variables: elements
```

We create a Vector with a given number of elements:

```
Vector class>>new: anInteger
     ^self new setElements: (Array new: anInteger)
Vector>>setElements: aCollection
     elements := aCollection
```

We'll ignore the arithmetic nature of Vectors and focus on how it delegates. Sometimes, clients want to treat a Vector as a Collection of Numbers. When someone iterates over a Vector, it delegates to its "elements" instance variable:

```
Vector>>do: aBlock
     elements do: aBlock
```

This is an example of Simple Delegation. You can imagine implementing at:, at:put:, size, etc. the same way.

Self Delegation

You are using Delegation (p. 64).

- How do you implement delegation to an object that needs reference to the delegating object?

The issues are the same for Self Delegation as for Simple Delegation. Do you need the identity of the original delegating object? Do you need state from the delegating object?

If the answer to either of these questions is "yes," Simple Delegation won't work. Somehow, the delegate needs access to the delegating object.

One way to give the delegate access is to include a reference from the delegate back to the delegating object. This approach has a number of drawbacks. The backwards reference introduces additional programming complexity. Every time the delegate changes, the reference in the old delegate has to be destroyed and the reference in the new delegate set. More importantly, each delegate can only be used by one delegating object at a time. If creating multiple copies of the delegate is expensive or impossible, this simply won't work.

The other approach, the one suggested here, is to pass the delegating object along as an additional parameter. This introduces a variant of the original method, which isn't great, but the additional flexibility of this approach is worth the cost.

- *Pass along the delegating object (i.e. "self") in an additional parameter called "for:"*

The Digitalk Visual Smalltalk 3.0 image has an excellent example of Self Delegation. The implementation of hashed collections, like Dictionaries, is divided into two parts. The first is the Dictionary, the second is a HashTable. There are variants of HashTables that are efficient in different circumstances. The same collection might delegate to different HashTables at different times, depending on its characteristics (how big, how full, etc.)

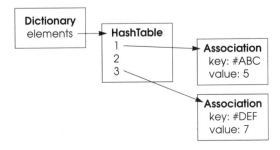

The hash value of an object is implemented differently for different kinds of Collections. Dictionaries compute hash by sending "hash." IdentityDictionaries compute it by sending "basicHash." This is implemented using Self Delegation. When the Collection sends a message to the HashTable to add an element, it passes itself along:

```
Dictionary>>at: keyObject put: valueObject
    self hashTable
        at: keyObject
        put: valueObject
        for: self
```

The HashTable computes the hash value by sending back a message to the Collection:

```
HashTable>>at: keyObject put: valueObject for: aCollection
    | hash |
    hash := aCollection hashOf: keyObject.
    ...
```

Dictionaries and IdentityDictionaries implement this message differently:

```
Dictionary>>hashOf: anObject
    ^anObject hash
IdentityDictionary>>hashOf: anObject
    ^anObject basicHash
```

Self Delegation allows the hierarchy of hashed Collections to be independent of the hierarchy of HashTables.

If the delegate needs different logic depending on who is delegating, use Double Dispatch (p. 55).

BACK

Pluggable Behavior

- How do you parameterize the behavior of an object?

The conventional model of objects is that different instances of the same class have different state and the same behavior. Every Point can have different values for x and y, but they all use the same logic to compute "translatedBy:." When you want different logic, you use a different class.

Using classes to specify behavior is simple. The programming tools are set up to help readers understand the behavior of your system statically, without necessarily having to run the code.

This model works for 90 percent of the objects you will create. Creating classes comes at a cost, though, and sometimes different classes don't effectively communicate how you think about a problem.

Classes are an opportunity. Each one will be useful to instantiate and/or specialize. However, each class you create places a burden on you, as the writer, to communicate its purpose and implementation to future readers. A system with hundreds or thousands of classes will intimidate a reader. Managing a namespace across many classes is expensive. You would like to invoke the costs of a new class only when there is a reasonable payoff. A large family of classes with only a single method each is unlikely to be valuable.

The other problem with specializing behavior only through classes is that classes are not flexible. Once you have created an object of a certain class, you cannot change that object's class without completely ruining the ability to understand the code statically. Only watching carefully while single stepping will give you insight into how such code runs. Smalltalk's single inheritance also does not allow specialization along several different axes at the same time.

If you are going to use Pluggable Behavior, here are the issues you need to consider:

- How much flexibility do you need?
- How many methods will need to vary dynamically?
- How hard is it to follow the code?

- Will clients need to specify the behavior to be plugged, or can it be hidden within the plugged object?

How can you specify different logic in different instances when creating lots of little classes or changing classes at run time won't work?

- *Add a variable that will be used to trigger different behavior.*

Typical examples of pluggable behavior are objects that have to interface with a variety of other objects, like user interface components that have to display the contents of many different objects. Using Pluggable Behavior is a much better solution than creating a hundred different subclasses, each differing from each other in only one or two methods.

For simple behavior changes, use a Pluggable Selector (p. 70). A Pluggable Block (p. 73) gives you more flexibility. Hide the implementation of pluggability behind an Intention Revealing Message (p. 48).

Pluggable Selector

You need simple Pluggable Behavior (p. 69).

- How do you code simple instance specific behavior?

The simplest way to implement Pluggable Behavior is to store a selector to be performed.

Let's say we have implemented a ListPane. We create a method that takes one of the elements of the collection to be displayed and returns a String:

```
ListPane>>printElement: anObject
    ^anObject printString
```

After awhile, we notice that there are many subclasses of ListPane that only override this one method:

```
     DollarListPane>>printElement: anObject
          ^anObject asDollarFormatString
     DescriptionListPane>>printElement: anObject
          ^anObject description
```

It hardly seems worth the cost of all these subclasses if all they are going to do is override one method. A simpler solution is to make ListPane itself a little more flexible, so different instances send different messages to their elements. We add a variable called "printMessage" and modify #printElement:

```
     ListPane>>printElement: anObject
          ^anObject perform: printMessage
```

To preserve the previous behavior, we would have to initialize the printMessage:

```
     ListPane>>initialize
          printMessage := #printString
```

Pluggable Selector meets the Pluggable Behavior criteria as follows:

Readability—Pluggable Selector is harder to follow than simple class-based behavior. By looking at an object with an inspector, you can tell how it will behave. You don't necessarily have to single step through the code.

Flexibility—The methods for the Pluggable Selectors must be implemented in the receiving object. The set of possible methods to be invoked should change at the same rate as the rest of the object.

Extent—Pluggable selectors should be used no more than twice per object. Any more than that and you risk obscuring the intent of the program. Use State Object if you need more dimensions of variability.

- *Add a variable that contains a selector to be performed. Append "Message" to the Role Suggesting Instance Variable Name. Create a Composed Method that simply performs the selector.*

Pluggable Selector is also useful for a simple kind of constraint. For example, if you wanted to locate one visual component relative to some part of another, we could use Pluggable Selector to create a RelativePoint:

```
Class: RelativePoint
    superclass: Object
    instance variables: figure locationMessage
```

Here is the Constructor Method:

```
RelativePoint class>>centered: aFigure
    ^self new
        setFigure: aFigure
        message: #center
RelativePoint>>setFigure: aFigure message: aSymbol
    figure := aFigure.
    locationMessage := aSymbol
```

To use a RelativePoint, you send it messages like #x and #y, just like a regular Point.

```
RelativePoint>>asPoint
    ^figure perform: locationMessage
RelativePoint>>x
    ^self asPoint x
```

Once you have this, you can go crazy duplicating all the necessary Point protocol, re-engineering for performance, etc. As an example of Pluggable Selector, however, the interesting observation is that you don't have to make a subclass for CenteredRelativePoint, TopLeftRelativePoint, etc.; you can capture the variability in a single selector.

Pluggable Block

You need complex Pluggable Behavior (p. 69) that is not implemented by the plugged object.

- How do you code complex Pluggable Behavior that is not quite worth its own class?

Pluggable Selector works when the behavior to be invoked lives within the plugged object. Sometimes, though, the behavior can't live within the plugged object either because it is complex and not related to the plugged object's other responsibilities, because it is already implemented in another object not easily accessible to the plugged object, or because the range of behavior to be plugged was not known when the object was created.

The common solution in this case, particularly when the behavior is already implemented, is to plug in a Block to be evaluated rather than a selector to be performed. The block can be created anywhere, can access objects otherwise inaccessible to the plugged object through the use of a Block Closure, and can involve arbitrary amounts of logic.

Blocks used in such a general way come at enormous cost. You can never statically analyze the code to understand the flow of control. Even inspecting the plugged object is unlikely to unearth its secrets. Only by single stepping through the invocation of the block will the reader understand what is going on.

Blocks are also more difficult to store on external media than Symbols. Some Object Streams and object databases cannot store and retrieve Blocks.

- *Add an instance variable to store a Block. Append "Block" to the Role Suggesting Instance Variable Name. Create a Composed Method to evaluate the Block to invoke the Pluggable Behavior.*

The VisualWorks object PluggableAdaptor is a good example of a Pluggable Block. All the objects in the ValueModel family, of which

PluggableAdaptor is one, provide the protocol #value and #value:. PluggableAdaptor implements these messages with a PluggableBlock. Here is a simplified implementation:

```
Class: PluggableAdaptor
    superclass: ValueModel
    instance variables: getBlock setBlock
```

The Constructor Method sets the blocks:

```
PluggableAdaptor class>>getBlock: getBlock setBlock:
setBlock
    ^self new
        setGetBlock: getBlock
        setBlock: setBlock
```

Notice that the Constructor Parameter Method has to use a variant of Type Suggesting Parameter Name because the obvious parameter names are already used for instance variable names.

```
PluggableAdaptor>>setGetBlock: gBlock setBlock: sBlock
    getBlock := gBlock.
    setBlock := sBlock
```

We can implement #value and #value: by invoking the Pluggable Blocks.

```
PluggableAdaptor>>value
    ^getBlock value
PluggableAdaptor>>value: anObject
    putBlock value: anObject
```

Now we can connect any object that expects #value and #value: to any other object:

```
Car>>speedAdaptor
    ^PluggableAdaptor
        getBlock: [self speed]
        putBlock: [:newSpeed | self speed: newSpeed]
```

Collecting Parameter

You have written an Intention Revealing Selector (p. 49).

- How do you return a collection that is the collaborative result of several methods?

One of the downsides of Composed Method is that it occasionally creates problems because of linkages between the small methods. A state that would have been stored in a temporary variable now has to be shared between methods.

The simplest solution to this problem is to leave all the code in a single method and use temporary variables to communicate between the parts of the method. All the benefits you expect from Composed Method vanish if you take this approach. The code is less revealing, more difficult to reuse and refine, and harder to modify.

Another solution is to add an instance variable to the object that is shared only between the methods. This variable is very different than the other variables in the object. It is only valid while the methods are executing, not for the lifetime of the object. Instance variables should exist to communicate and store only state that must go together.

We can solve the problem by adding an additional parameter that is passed to all the methods. I hesitate to add layers of methods like this, except when they do useful work. In this case, because the other solutions aren't valid, this is the right solution.

● *Add a parameter that collects their results to all of the submethods.*

Here's an example. The following code extracts all the married men and unmarried women from a collection of people:

```
marriedMenAndUnmarriedWomen
    | result |
    result := OrderedCollection new.
    self people do: [:each | each isMarried & each isMan
ifTrue: [result add: each]].
    self people do: [:each | each isUnmarried & each
isWoman ifTrue: [result add: each]].
    ^result
```

Using Composed Method, we put each iteration into its own method:

```
marriedMen
    | result |
    result := OrderedCollection new.
    self people do: [:each | each isMarried & each isMan
ifTrue: [result add: each]].
    ^result
unmarriedWomen
    | result |
    result := OrderedCollection new.
    self people do: [:each | each isUnmarried & each
isWoman ifTrue: [result add: each]].
    ^result
```

Now the question is how to compose the two methods. For an example this simple, I would probably use Concatenation to write:

```
marriedMenAndUnmarriedWomen
    ^self marriedMen , self unmarriedWomen
```

but that doesn't demonstrate this pattern very well. If several layers of methods, or several objects, are involved, it is more clear to modify the submethods. Instead of returning a Collection, each adds its objects to a Collection. The code then becomes:

```
marriedMenAndUnmarriedWomen
    | result |
    result := OrderedCollection new.
    self addMarriedMenTo: result.
    self addUnmarriedWomenTo: result.
    ^result
addMarriedMenTo: aCollection
    self people do: [:each | each isMarried & each isMan
ifTrue: [aCollection add: each]]
addUnmarriedWomenTo: aCollection
    self people do: [:each | each isUnmarried & each
isWoman ifTrue: [aCollection add: each]]
```

This code contains fewer lines and is more direct than the original. (If this were production code, I would probably continue factoring via Composed Method to concentrate the similarities between addMarriedMenTo: and addUnmarriedWomenTo:.)

In general, use an OrderedCollection (p. 116) as the Collecting Parameter. You may use a Concatenating Stream (p. 165) as the Collecting Parameter if the objects to be collected are bytes or Characters. Use a Set (p. 119) if you want to avoid duplicates.

Chapter 4

State

Sure, how you specify behavior is most important in coding Smalltalk objects, but you still won't get anywhere without state. Before you start a computation, something has to record what the problem is. While you are computing, you often need to store intermediate results. When you finish a computation, you have to remember the answer.

Most state-related decisions have more to do with modeling and less with coding, so the patterns here don't tell anything like the whole story. However, the tactical decisions you make about representation will have an important impact on how well your code communicates with others.

This section talks about two kinds of state: instance variables and temporary variables. Of the two, temporary variables are covered much more thoroughly because they are a complete artifact of coding, living only as long as a method is computing. Instance variables also have an important role to play in coding, however, so their role in coding, and even some of their roles in modeling, is covered here.

Instance Variables

I wrote the section on Temporary Variables before I wrote this section. I was pleased with how the section on temps came out. I expected this section to turn out to be the same sort of cut-and-dry, "Here's how it goes" list of patterns. It didn't.

The problem is that temporary variables really are all about coding. They are a tactical solution to a tactical problem. Thus, they fit very well in the scope of this book.

Most uses of instance variables are not tactical. Along with the distribution of computational responsibility, the choice of how to represent a model is at the core of modeling. The decision to create an instance variable usually comes from a much different mind-set and in a different context than the decision to create a temp.

I leave this section here because there are still important coding reasons to create instance variables, and there are some practical, tactical techniques to be learned when using instance variables.

Common State

- How do you represent state, different values for which will exist in all instances of a class?

In the dawn of computing time, state was all there was. What is a box of punched cards but a bunch of state made manifest? Unit record equipment existed to re-order and transform the state, but all the transformations were hard-coded (like with wires and pulleys and gears) into the machines. State was king.

The first thing electronic computing did was make state virtual. No longer did it only exist in physical form, that physical form was turned into electrons so it could be more easily and quickly manipulated. The manipulations were still physically manifested in the form of patch cords, but they were getting easier to change.

The stored program computer changed all this. Now, the manipulations and the state were on par. They were both virtual parts of the same machine, stored as charges that could easily be changed.

Because of the extreme resource limitations of those early machines, the unification of program and state became complete. You could encode a program in fewer bytes if you were willing to treat it like data sometimes—

changing the program as circumstances changed. Of course, you could never hope to just read program source and understand what was happening, you had to watch the program in action under lots of different conditions before you understood it.

Once we had enough memory that we no longer needed to commit atrocities in the name of space efficiency, state still bit us on the backside. Huge programs were written where many many functions used many many different bits of state. No part of the state could be changed without changing many parts of the program.

The enormous cost of such programs led to a backlash. Programs as state were bad. State must be bad, too. This led to the development of functional programming, where there is no state, only programs.

In spite of their conceptual and mathematical elegance, functional programming languages never caught on for commercial software. The problem is that programmers think and model in terms of state. State is a pretty darn good way to think about the world.

Objects represent a middle ground. State is good, but only when properly managed. It is manageable if it is chopped into little pieces, some alike and some different. Similarly, related programs are chopped into little pieces, some alike, some different. That way, changing part of the representation of the state of a program need lead to only a few, localized changes in the program.

● *Declare an instance variable in the class.*

A Cartesian Point has instance variables to hold its horizontal and vertical offsets. A Point in polar coordinates has instance variables to hold its radius and angular offset. A House has an instance variable to hold a collection of all of its rooms.

Instance variables have a very important communicative role to play. They say once and for all and out in the open, "Here's what I'm modeling with this object." A set of objects reveals a lot that was in the mind of the original programmer just by what the instance variables are and what they are named.

Be sure to declare instance variables in order of importance in the class definition.

Name the variable using Role Suggesting Instance Variable Name (p. 110). Initialize the instance variable either with Lazy Initialization (p. 85), Explicit Initialization (p. 83), or a Constructor Parameter Method (p. 25). You need to choose whether to use the variable with Direct Variable Access (p. 89) or Indirect Variable Access (p. 91).

Variable State

- How do you represent state whose presence varies from instance to instance?

Warning! This is not a pattern you should use often, if ever. It is here because you will see code written with it and you will have to understand what is going on.

This pattern is here for all the LISP programmers who come to Smalltalk. Some LISP cultures value flexibility over all else. Their objects tend to have no fixed parts. A Point might have an x, it might have a y, it might have a color, who knows?

The symptom of code like this is that classes declare a single instance variable that holds a Dictionary mapping of Strings or Symbols (the names of variables) to Objects. Some of the values of the Dictionary might be Numbers, others Collections, others Strings. Moreover, if you look at several instances of this class, all of their Dictionaries have the same keys.

The problem with code like this is that you can't read it and understand what is going on. The programming tools don't support this style of programming well. There is no equivalent of "browse instance variable references" for code that stores all its state in Dictionaries.

It is certainly legitimate to build models where state is sometimes present and sometimes not, even in instances of the same class. You wouldn't want to declare a hundred variables, almost all of which are nil in almost all instances, just because a few instances will need them.

- *Put variables that only some instances will have in a Dictionary stored in an instance variable called "properties." Implement "propertyAt: aSymbol" and "propertyAt: aSymbol put: anObject" to access properties.*

Visual Smalltalk uses properties connected to its graphical widgets to communicate between various parts of the program. For example, an EntryField has a property called 'PreviousContents,' which is used to determine whether the field's contents have changed.

VisualWorks 2.5 has a perfect example of when NOT to use this pattern. Their Package object uses Variable State. The Constructor Method takes a name for the Package, so every Package has to have a name (Common State, right?). However, instead of being stored in an instance variable, it is stored as part of the Variable State.

Make sure that with any variables, all or nearly all instances shared are implemented as instance variables, not as entries on the property list. Variable State is often used as a temporary convenience and never revisited, even though its generality is not used.

You may want to hide the difference between variables stored as instance variables and variables stored on the property list with a Getting Method (p. 93) and Setting Method (p 95).

Explicit Initialization

You've found Common State (p. 80) that always starts at the same value. A Constructor Parameter Method (p. 25) has just set the state of some variables.

- How do you initialize instance variables to their default value?

Usually, in these patterns, I have tried to avoid ambiguity. If there are two equally valid ways to accomplish some task, I pick one.

Initialization is an issue for which I cannot in good conscience pick one solution. There are two ways to solve the problem of instance variable initialization, each valid in different circumstances—circumstances you are certain to encounter.

This pattern emphasizes readability over flexibility. You should use an initialize method when you want people to read your code as easily as possible and you aren't terribly concerned about future subclasses. By putting all the initialization in one place, Explicit Initialization makes it easy to figure out what all the variables are.

Flexibility is impaired by Explicit Initialization because all of the variables are mentioned in a single method. If you add or remove an instance variable, you will have to remember to edit the Explicit Initialization.

Explicit Initialization can also be more costly than Lazy Initialization Methods because they spend the effort to initialize all the values at instance creation time. If computing some of the initial values is expensive and the values aren't used right away (or perhaps not at all), you may be able to improve performance by not initializing them right away.

- *Implement a method "initialize" that sets all the values explicitly. Override the class message "new" to invoke it on new instances.*

For example, consider a Timer that defaults to executing every 1000 milliseconds. It also keeps track of how many times it has gone off:

```
Class: Timer
    superclass: Object
    instance variables: period count
```

Use basicNew to create the instance to avoid accidentally setting "initialize" off twice, should a future superclass invoke it.

```
Timer class>>new
    ^self basicNew initialize
```

Now we can initialize the values:

```
Timer>>initialize
    count := 0.
    period := 1000
```

Even better, we can explain that magic number 1000 with a message:

```
Timer>>defaultMillisecondPeriod
    ^1000
Timer>>initialize
    count := 0.
    period := self defaultMillisecondPeriod
```

Put #initialize methods in a method protocol called "initialize-release."

Use Default Value Method (p. 86) to explain any value that isn't obvious. Initialize Methods in a hierarchy commonly need Extending Super (p. 60) to finish their job.

Lazy Initialization

You are initializing Common State (p. 80).

- How do you initialize an instance variable to its default value?

Here is the flip side of variable initialization. All the strengths of Explicit Initialization become weaknesses and all the weaknesses strengths.

Lazy Initialization breaks initialization into two methods per variable. The first is a Getting Method that hides the fact that the variable is lazily initialized from anyone wanting to use its value. This implies that there can be no Direct Variable Access. The second method, the Default Value Method, provides the default value of the variable.

This is where the flexibility comes in. If you make a subclass, you can change the default value by overriding the Default Value Method.

Readability suffers because there isn't any one place you can look to see all the variables and their initial values. Instead, you have to look at several methods to see all the values.

Performance is another reason to use a Lazy Initialization. Expensive initialization that may not be needed for a while (or at all) can be deferred by using Lazy Initialization.

- *Write a Getting Method for the variable. Initialize it if necessary with a Default Value Method.*

The Timer example from above needs no explicit initialization. Instead, count is initialized in its Getting Method:

```
Timer>>count
    count isNil ifTrue: [count := self defaultCount].
    ^count
```

The default value comes from its own method:

```
Timer>>defaultCount
    ^0
```

Similarly for period:

```
Timer>>period
    period isNil ifTrue: [period := self defaultPeriod].
    ^period
Timer>>defaultPeriod
    ^1000
```

Some people swear by Lazy Initialization. They go so far as to say that all initialization should be done this way. I actually lean towards Explicit Initialization. Too many times, I've bent over backwards to supply lots of flexibility that is never used. I'd rather do it the simple way first, then fix it if it's a problem. However, if I know I am writing code that is likely to be subclassed by others, I'll go ahead and use Lazy Initialization from the first.

A Default Value Method (p. 86) supplies a default value. A Compute Method supplies the value of a Caching Instance Variable.

Default Value Method

You have a complicated default value in Explicit Initialization (p. 83). You need a default value for Lazy Initialization (p. 85).

- How do you represent the default value of a variable?

    The simplest way to provide default values is right in line with the code. It's generally easy to read and quick and simple to write.

Patterns whose purpose is creating flexibility (Lazy Initialization) or who may need additional communication (Explicit Initialization), need an Intention Revealing Message. It gives you an opportunity to communicate through the selector. It gives future subclasses the option of simply overriding a single value.

• *Create a method that returns the value. Prepend "default" to the name of the variable as the name of the method.*

A Book might offer up an empty String as its synopsis if no synopsis has been entered:

```
Book>>defaultSynopsis
    ^"
```

If you are computing the value of a Caching Instance Variable, call the method "computeArea" rather than "defaultArea." This will provide a clue to readers that the variable is intended as a cache.

Put Default Value Methods in a method protocol called "private."

Use a Constant Method (p. 87) for constant default values.

Constant Method

You are writing a Composed Method (p. 21). You may need a Default Value Method (p. 86).

• How do you code a constant?

Smalltalk provides several options for representing shared constants or variables. Pools provide a set of variables that can be used in any number of different classes. Class variables are variables that are shared throughout a hierarchy.

I know that some folks use lots of pools in their applications. I never use them. Here's what I don't like about pools—they make it too easy to stop making useful responsibilities and instead just spread data around.

The IBM Smalltalk window system is a good example. There is a pool called CwConstants that contains hundreds of constants. Rather than being able to send a list pane a message like #singleSelect to make it select one item at a time, you send it "selectionPolicy: XmSINGLESELECT."

Of course, you could say that this is just one little thing you have to remember, and besides, C programmers have to deal with stuff like this all the time. However, multiply "one little thing to remember" by several hundred and you don't have a system that feels much like Smalltalk any more, at least not when you're working with the window system.

I would rather limit the visibility of constants to a single class. Then, that class can provide meaningful behavior to other objects. If you can refactor your code so that only a single class cares about a constant, you can then represent that constant as a method.

In the list pane example, this means leaving the original implementation of #selectionPolicy: alone but not expecting outside objects to invoke it. Instead, for each of the possible argument values we create a method:

```
ListPane>>singleSelect
    self selectionPolicy: 15
```

If other methods also needed to know that 15 was the magic constant for single selection, we create a method for it—a method that just returns 15.

```
ListPane>>singleSelectPolicy
    ^15
ListPane>>singleSelect
    self selectionPolicy: self singleSelectPolicy
```

One of the downsides of representing constants as methods is it is easier to automatically generate the initialization for a pool than it is to automatically create a method. If you have to synchronize a set of constants with other programs, you may find it easier to use pools. However, you should still strive to provide rich protocol so that few classes need to know about the pool.

Another question about Constant Methods is what happens when you have hundreds or thousands of constants? A pool can easily grow to contain as many entries as necessary. A class with a thousand Constant Methods would look cluttered.

- *Create a method that returns the constant.*

You can implement the colors of visual components as Constant Methods:

```
SelectorFigure>>textColor
    ^Color darkGray
ExpressionFigure>>textColor
    ^Color chartreuse
```

A comment I've heard over and over about this pattern is, "What if you have to deal with hundreds of constants in one class?" To me, a class that has to deal with hundreds of constants is almost certainly doing too much work and needs to be broken up. However, if you absolutely have to, you can use other facilities like Pools to manage huge numbers of shared constants.

Put Constant Methods in a method protocol called "private."

Direct Variable Access

You need to access Common State (p. 80) as readably as possible.

How do you get and set an instance variable's value?

Accessing state is a topic much like initialization. There are two good answers. One is more readable. One is more flexible. Also like initialization, you will find dogmatic adherents of both approaches.

The simple, readable way to get and set the values of instance variables is to use the variables directly in all the methods that need their values. The alternative requires that you send a message every time you need to use or change an instance variable's value.

When I first started programming in Smalltalk, at Tektronix in the mid-80s, the debate about accessing state was hot. There were factions on both sides making self-important statements (don't you just love research labs?)

The Indirect Variable Access crowd has won the hearts and mind of the Smalltalking public, mostly, I think, because most of the high volume training companies teach indirect access. The issue is nowhere near as simple as "direct access bad, indirect access good."

I tried to reopen the debate in my Smalltalk Report column a few years back. A little brush fire started that eventually fizzled out. I was wondering if I was making too big a deal of the merits of direct access. Maybe I should have left well enough alone.

Then, I spent several months working for a client that insisted on indirect access. A professional programmer can take on any of a number of styles at will, so I was a good soldier and wrote my getters and setters.

After I was done with that client, I wrote some code for myself. I was amazed at how much smoother it read than what I had been previously working on. The only difference in style was direct versus indirect access.

What I noticed was that every time I read:

```
...self x...
```

I paused for a moment to remind myself that the message "x" was just fetching an instance variable. When I read:

```
...x...
```

I just kept reading.

I told Ward of my experience. He had another good explanation. When you write classes that only have a handful of methods, adding a getting and a setting method can easily double the number of methods in your class—twice as many methods to buy you flexibility that you may never use.

On the other hand, it's awful frustrating to get a class from someone and see the opportunity to quickly subclass it, only to discover that they used Direct Variable Access, so there is no way to make the changes you want without changing most of the code in the superclass.

- *Access and set the variable directly.*

Most of the example code in this book uses Direct Variable Access because I want to be as easy to read as possible. When you have direct access, putting in Indirect Variable Access is no big deal. Thus, you can read:

```
Point>>setX: xNumber y: yNumber
    x := xNumber.
    y := yNumber
```

quickly, and there is no danger that you won't know what to do if you choose indirect access later.

Indirect Variable Access

BACK

You need to access Common State (p. 80) as flexibly as possible.

How do you get and set an instance variable's value?

Now I have to display my true schizophrenia. Having convinced you in Direct Variable Access that just using variables is good enough, I'm going to ask you to ignore that crazy bastard and listen to me talk some sense here.

When you use Direct Variable Access, many methods make the assumption that a variable's value is valid. For some code this is a reasonable assumption. However, if you want to introduce Lazy Initialization, to stop storing and start computing the value, or if you want to change assumptions in a new subclass, you will be disappointed that the assumption of validity is wide spread.

The solution is to always use Getting Methods and Setting Methods to access variables. Thus, instead of:

```
Point>>+ aPoint
    ^x + aPoint x @ (y + aPoint y)
```

you would see:

```
Point>>+ aPoint
    ^self x + aPoint x @ (self y @ aPoint y)
```

If you browse the instance variable references of a class that uses Indirect Variable Access, you will only see two references to each variable, the Getting Method and the Setting Method.

What you give up with Indirect Variable Access is simplicity and readability. You have to define all those Getting Methods and Setting Methods. Even if you have your system do it for you, you have that many more methods to manage and document. As explained above, code using Direct Variable Access reads smoothly because you are not forever reminding yourself "Oh yeah, that's just a Getting Method."

- *Access and set its value only through a Getting Method and Setting Method.*

A Point written with Indirect Variable Access provides methods for its instance variables:

```
Point>>x
    ^x
Point>>x: aNumber
    x := aNumber
```

That way, you could define a PolarPoint subclass that merely implemented these methods differently, and all the superclass code would still work.

```
PolarPoint>>x
    ^self radius cos * self theta
```

If you need to code for inheritance, use Indirect Variable Access. Future generations will thank you.

One warning—do not go half way. If you are going to use direct access, use it for all access. If you decide later you need to move a variable to indirect access, perhaps to take advantage of Lazy Initialization, change the accessing of the variable throughout. On the other hand, it doesn't bother me much to see some variables in an object accessed directly and others indirectly.

You will need to define a Getting Method (p. 93) and a Setting Method (p. 95) for each variable. For variables holding collections, consider implementing Collection Accessor Methods (p. 96) and an Enumeration Method (p. 144).

Getting Method

You are using Lazy Initialization or Indirect Variable Access (p. 91).

- How do you provide access to an instance variable?

Once you have decided to use Indirect Variable Access, you are committed to providing a message-based protocol for getting and setting variable values. The only real questions are how you use it and what you call it.

Here's the real secret of writing good Getting Methods—***make them private at first***. I cannot stress this enough. You will be fine if the same object invokes and implements the Getting Method. Another way of saying this is you always send messages invoking Getting Methods to "self."

Some people try to ensure this by prefixing "my" to the name of the method. Thus, instead of:

```
x
    ^x
```

you have:

```
myX
    ^x
```

This makes sure that code like:

```
self bounds origin myX
```

looks stupid. I don't feel this is necessary. I'd rather give programmers (myself included) the benefit of the doubt. If some other object absolutely has to send my private Getting Method, it should be able to do so in as readable a manner as possible.

- *Provide a method that returns the value of the variable. Give it the same name as the variable.*

A Book that needed to display its author and title in a user interface would publish Getting Methods:

```
Book>>author
        ^author
Book>>title
        ^title
```

There are cases where you will publish the existence of Getting Methods for use in the outside world. You should make a conscious decision to do this after considering all the alternatives. It is preferable to give an object more responsibility, rather than have it act like a data structure.

Put private Getting Methods in a method protocol called "private-accessing." Put public Getting Methods in a method protocol called "accessing."

Setting Method

BACK

You are using Indirect Variable Access (p. 91).

- How do you change the value of an instance variable?

Everything I said once about Getting Methods, I'd like to say twice about Setting Methods. Setting Methods should be even more private. It is one thing for another object to tear out your state, it is quite another for it to bash in a new state. The possibilities for the code in the two objects to get out of sync and break, in confusing ways, are legion.

Revisiting naming, I don't feel it is necessary to prepend "my" to the names of Setting Methods. It might provide a little more protection from unauthorized use, but I don't think the extra difficulty reading is worth it.

- *Provide a method with the same name as the variable. Have it take a single parameter, the value to be set.*

A Book editing interface would need Setting Methods for author and title:

```
Book>>author: aString
    author := aString
Book>>title: aString
    title := aString
```

Even if I use Indirect Variable Access, if I have a variable that is only set at instance creation time, I would not provide a Setting Method. I'd use the Constructor Parameter Method to set the all the values at once. Once you have a Setting Method, though, you should use it for all changes to the variable.

Put private Setting Methods in a method protocol called "private-accessing." Put public Setting Methods in a method protocol called "accessing."

Set boolean properties with a Boolean Property Setting Method (p. 100).

Collection Accessor Method

You are using Indirect Variable Access (p. 91).

- How do you provide access to an instance variable that holds a collection?

The simplest solution is just to publish a Getting Method for the variable. That way, any client that wants can add to, delete from, iterate over, or otherwise use the collection.

The problem with this approach is that it opens up too much of the implementation of an object to the outside world. If the object decides to change the implementation, say by using a different kind of collection, the client code may well break.

The other problem with just offering up your private collections for public viewing is that it is hard to keep related state current when someone else is changing the collection without notifying you. Here's a department that uses a Caching Instance Variable to speed access to its total salary:

```
Department
        superclass: Object
        instance variables: employees totalSalary
totalSalary
        totalSalary isNil ifTrue: [totalSalary := self computeTotalSalary].
        ^totalSalary
computeTotalSalary
        ^employees
                inject: 0
                into: [:sum :each | sum + each salary]
clearTotalSalary
        totalSalary := nil
```

What happens if client code deletes an employee without notifying the department?

```
...aDepartment employees remove: anEmployee...
```

The totalSalary cache never gets cleared. It now contains a number inconsistent with the value returned by computeTotalSalary.

The solution to this is not to let other objects have your collections. If you use Indirect Variable Access, make sure Getting Methods for collections are private. Instead, give clients restricted access to operations on the collection through messages that you implement. This gives you a chance to do whatever other processing you need to.

The downside of this approach is that you have to actually implement all of these methods. Giving access to a collection takes one method. You might need four or five methods to provide all the necessary protected access to the collection. In the long run, it's worth it though, because your code will read better and be easier to change.

- *Provide methods that are implemented with Delegation to the collection. To name the methods, add the name of the collection to the collection messages.*

If Department wanted to let others add and delete employees, it would implement Collection Accessor Methods:

```
addEmployee: anEmployee
    self clearTotalSalary.
    employees add: anEmployee
removeEmployee: anEmployee
    self clearTotalSalary.
    employees remove: anEmployee
```

Don't just blindly name a Collection Accessor Method after the collection message it delegates. See if you can find a word from the domain that makes more sense. For example, I prefer:

```
employs: anEmployee
    ^employees includes: anEmployee
```

to:

```
includesEmployee: anEmployee
    ^employees includes: anEmployee
```

FORWARD

Put Collection Accessor Methods in a method protocol called "accessing."

Implement an Enumeration Method (p. 99) for safe and efficient general collection access.

Enumeration Method

BACK

You are using Indirect Variable Access (p. 91). You may have implemented a Collection Accessor Method (p. 96).

● How do you provide safe, general access to collection elements?

Sometimes, clients want lots of ways of accessing a private collection. You could implement twenty or thirty Collection Accessor Methods but you haven't the time and you aren't even sure even that would be enough. At the same time, all the arguments for not just making a Getting Method for the collection public still hold.

● *Implement a method that executes a Block for each element of the collection. Name the method by concatenating the name of the collection and "Do:."*

The Enumeration Method for a Department's Employees looks like this:

```
Department>>employeesDo: aBlock
    employees do: aBlock
```

Now client code that wants to get a collection of all of the Employees in a bunch of departments can use a Concatenating Stream:

```
allEmployees
    | writer |
    writer := WriteStream on: Array new.
    self departments do: [:eachDepartment |
eachDepartment employeesDo: [:eachEmployee | writer
nextPut: eachEmployee]]
        ^writer contents
```

What if you want Departments to be able to contain other Departments, and not just Employees (this is an example of the modeling pattern Composite)? You can implement employeesDo: for both:

```
Department>>employeesDo: aBlock
    employees do: [:each | each employeesDo: aBlock]
Employee>>employeesDo: aBlock
    aBlock value: self
```

Put Enumeration Methods in a method protocol called "enumerating."

Boolean Property Setting Method

You are using a Setting Method (p. 95).

- How do you set a boolean property?

The simplest solution is to use a Setting Method. Let's say we have a Switch that stores a Boolean in an instance variable "isOn." The Setting Method is:

```
Switch>>on: aBoolean
        isOn := aBoolean
```

There are two problems with this approach. The first is that it exposes the representation of the status of the switch to clients. This has led me to situations where I make a representation change in one object that has to be reflected in many others. The second problem is that it is hard to answer simple questions like "who turns on the switch?"

Creating distinct methods for the two states causes you to create one more method than you would have otherwise. However, the cost of these methods is money well spent because of the improvement in communication of the resulting code.

Using the names of the two states as the names of the methods is tempting (Switch>>on and Switch>>off, in this example). As with Query Method, though, there is a potential confusion about whether you're interrogating the object or telling it what to do. Thus, even though adding another word to the selector results in a selector that is less natural to say, the added clarity is worth it.

- *Create two methods beginning with "be." One has property name, the other the negation. Add "toggle" if the client doesn't want to know about the current state.*

Here are some examples:

```
beVisible/beInvisible/toggleVisible
beDirty/beClean
```

Put Boolean Property Setting Methods in a method protocol called "accessing."

BACK

Role Suggesting Instance Variable Name

You need to name Common State (p. 80).

• What do you name an instance variable?

The two important pieces of information to communicate about any variable are:

• What is its purpose?

• How is it used?

The purpose or role of a variable is important to the reader because it helps direct their attention appropriately. Typically, when you read code you have a purpose in mind. If you understand the role of a variable and it is unrelated to your purpose, you can quickly skim over irrelevant code that uses that variable. Likewise, if you see a variable that is related to your purpose, you can quickly narrow your reading to relevant code by looking for that variable.

How a variable is used and the messages it is sent are its "type." Smalltalk doesn't have declared types, but that doesn't mean they aren't important. Understanding the messages sent to a variable tells you what objects can be safely placed as values in that variable. Substitution of objects is the heart of disciplined maintenance and reuse.

Different variables appear in different contexts, so what you need to communicate with their names is different. The context for instance variables is most similar to the context for temporary variables. The only way you have for communicating the role of an instance variable is through its name. If the variables in Point were called "t1" and "t2" instead of "x" and "y," you'd have a lot of reading to do before you could tell which was the horizontal component and which the vertical. Naming the variables by their roles gives you that information directly.

On the other hand, the type of an instance variable is easily discovered from the code in which it resides. It is easy to find where the variable is used and from there discover what messages it is sent. You also get hints from Creation Parameter Setting Methods or Setting Methods that set the value of the variable. If I asked you what the type of "x" was in:

```
Point>>x: aNumber
    x := aNumber
```

you'd be able to tell me instantly. In the interest of keeping names simple, short, and readable, you can safely leave out any mention of the type of a variable in its name.

- *Name instance variables for the role they play in the computation. Make the name plural if the variable will hold a Collection.*

The role of the instance variable "x" is to hold the horizontal offset of the Point. The role of the "y" instance variable is to hold the vertical offset.

Temporary Variables

Temporary variables let you store and reuse the value of expressions. They can be used to improve the performance or readability of methods. The following patterns motivate and guide the use of temporary variables. The examples are taken from Smalltalk, but the discussion applies to any language with procedure-scoped variables.

Temporary Variable

A Composed Method (p. 21) needs temporary storage.

- How do you save the value of an expression for later use within a method?

A stateless language like FP contains no notion whatever of a variable. If you need the value of an expression, you evaluate the expression. If you need it in many places in a program, you evaluate it many places.

While the abstract properties of a stateless language might be attractive to a language designer, practical programs use variables to simplify the expression of computation. Each variable has several distinguishing features. The scope of a variable is the textual area within which it can be used. The extent of a variable defines how long its value lasts. The type of a variable is the signature of messages sent to it.

Long extent, wide scope, and large type all make variables difficult to manage. If all three factors are present in many variables, you have a program that can only be understood in its entirety. Limiting the scope, extent, and type of variables wherever possible produces programs that are easier to understand, modify, and reuse.

Another language design decision is whether to require the explicit declaration of variables. Early languages, like FORTRAN, detected the presence of variables automatically. ALGOL and its descendants required explicit declaration. Explicit declaration puts a burden on the programmer writing the program but pays off when someone else needs to understand the program. The presence and use of variables is often the first place a reader begins.

- *Create a variable whose scope and extent is a single method. Declare it just below the method selector. Assign it as soon as the expression is valid.*

Temporary variables are good at helping you understand a computation that is halfway towards its goal. Thus, you can more easily read:

```
Rectangle>>bottomRight
    | right bottom |
    right := self left + self width.
    bottom := self top + self height.
    ^right @ bottom
```

than you can:

```
Rectangle>>bottomRight
    ^self left + self width @ (self top + self height)
```

Collecting Temporary Variable saves intermediate results for later use. Caching Temporary Variable (p. 106))improves performance by saving values. Explaining Temporary Variable (p. 108) improves readability by breaking up complex expressions. Reusing Temporary Variable (p. 109) lets you use the value of a side-effecting expression more than once in a method.

Collecting Temporary Variable

Sometimes a Temporary Variable (p. 103) is used to collect intermediate results.

- How do you gradually collect values to be used later in a method?

The right set of enumeration protocol would make this question moot. Inject:into:, in particular, often eliminates the need for a temporary variable. Code like:

```
| sum |
sum := 0.
self children do: [:each | sum := sum + each size].
^sum
```

can be rewritten as:

```
^self children
        inject: 0
        into: [:sum :each | sum + each size]
```

The variety of enumeration strategies in complex programs makes it impossible to generalize the inject:into: idiom. For example, what if you want to merge two collections together so that you have an element from collection a, an element from collection b, and so on. This would require a special enumeration method:

```
^self leftFingers
        with: self rightFingers
        inject: Array new
        into: [:sum :eachLeft :eachRight |
        ...(sum copyWith: eachLeft) copyWith: eachRight]
```

It is much simpler to create a Stream for the duration of the method:

```
| results |
results := Array new writeStream.
self leftFingers with: self rightFingers do:
    [:eachLeft :eachRight | results nextPut: eachLeft;
nextPut: eachRight].
    ^results contents
```

- *When you need to collect or merge objects over a complex enumeration, use a temporary variable to hold the collection or merged value.*

The variable "answer" in Collection>>deepCopy is a simple example of a Collecting Temporary Variable:

```
deepCopy
    | answer |
    answer := self species new.
    self do: [:each | answer add: each copy].
    ^answer
```

Role Suggesting Temporary Variable Name (p. 102) explains how to name the variable.

Caching Temporary Variable

A performance measurement has shown you that an expression in a method is a bottleneck.

- How do you improve the performance of a method?

Many performance related decisions sacrifice programming style to the needs of demanding users with limited machine resources. Successful performance tuning hinges on being explicitly aware of this tradeoff and only introducing changes that pay back in increased performance more than they cost in increased maintenance.

As with variables, the scope and extent of a performance tuning decision dramatically affect its cost. Performance related changes that are confined to a single object are good, changes that only affect a single method are even better.

All performance tuning boils down to two techniques—either you execute code less often or you execute code that costs less. Of these, the first is often the most valuable. It relies on the fact that for reasons of readability, expressions are often executed several times even though they return the same value. Caching saves the value of the expression so that the next time the value is used instantly.

The biggest problem with caches is their assumption that the expression returns the same value. What if this isn't true? What if it is true for a while, but then the value of the expression changes? You can limit the complexity introduced by the need to keep a cache valid by limiting the scope and extent of the variable used for the cache.

- *Set a temporary variable to the value of the expression as soon as it is valid. Use the variable instead of the expression in the remainder of the method.*

For example, you might have some graphics code that uses the bounds of the receiver. If calculating the bounds is expensive, you can transform:

```
self children do: [:each | ...self bounds...]
```

into:

```
| bounds |
bounds := self bounds.
self children do: [:each | ...bounds...]
```

If the cost of calculating the bounds dominates the cost of the method, this takes a method that is linear in cost in the number of children and turns it into one that is constant.

Role Suggesting Temporary Variable Name (p. 102) explains how to name the variable. Caching Instance Variable caches expression values if they are used from many methods.

Explaining Temporary Variable

Temporary Variable (p. 103) can be used to improve the readability of complex methods.

- How do you simplify a complex expression within a method?

In the passion of the moment, you can write expressions within methods that are quite complex. Most expressions are simple at first. As soon as you are looking at live data, though, you realize your naive assumptions will never work. You add this complexity, then that one, then another, until you have many layers of messages piled on each other. While you are debugging, it is all understandable because you have so much context. Coming back to such a method in six months is quite a different experience.

Fixing the method right might require changes to several objects. While you are just exploring, such a commitment might be inappropriate.

- *Take a subexpression out of the complex expression. Assign its value to a temporary variable before the complex expression. Use the variable instead in the complex expression.*

An example is the use of the variable "lastIndex" in LinearHashTable>>findKeyIndex:for: from Visual Smalltalk. The message "size" is fast, so the performance of the method would probably not change much if the variable weren't used. The size of the receiver is being used to mean a final value for an index, so the variable helps explain the method:

```
LinearHashTable>>findKeyIndex: element for: client
    | index indexedObject lastIndex |
    lastIndex := self size.
    ...
```

Role Suggesting Temporary Variable Name (p. 102) explains how to name the variable. Composed Method (p. 21) puts the subexpression where it belongs and gives it a name.

Reusing Temporary Variable

Temporary Variable (p. 103) can be used to reuse the value of expressions that cannot be executed more than once.

- How do you use an expression several places in a method when its value may change?

Methods without temporary variables are easier to understand than methods with temporary variables. However, you sometimes encounter expressions whose values change, either because of side-effects of evaluating the expression or because of outside effects, but you need to use the value more than once. Using a temporary variable is worth the cost in such a case, because the code simply wouldn't work otherwise.

For example, if you are reading from a stream, the evaluation of "stream next" causes the stream to change. If you are matching the value read against a list of keywords, you must save the value. Thus:

```
stream next = a ifTrue: [...].
stream next = b ifTrue: [...].
stream next = c ifTrue: [...]
```

is not likely what you mean. Instead, you need to save the value in a temporary variable so you only execute "stream next" once.

```
| token |
token := stream next.
token = a ifTrue: [...]
...
```

Resources that are affected by the outside world also require this treatment. For example, "Time millisecondClockValue" cannot be executed more than once if you want to be guaranteed the same answer.

- *Execute the expression once and set a temporary variable. Use the variable instead of the expression in the remainder of the method.*

Role Suggesting Temporary Variable Name (p. 110) explains how to name the variable.

Role Suggesting Temporary Variable Name

Collecting Temporary Variable (p. 105) stores the intermediate results of a computation. Caching Temporary Variable (p. 106) improves performance by eliminating redundant computation. Explaining Temporary Variable (p. 108) makes methods containing complex expressions easier to read. Reusing Temporary Variable (p. 109) correctly executes methods containing side-effecting expressions.

- What do you call a temporary variable?

There are two important dimensions to communicate about a variable. The first is its type. Readers wishing to modify code need to know what responsibilities are assumed for an object occupying a variable. The second important dimension is role, that is, how the object is used in the computation. Understanding the role is important to understanding the method in which the variable is used. Different kinds of variables require different naming treatments to communicate type and role.

Temporary variables communicate their role by context. If you are staring at:

```
| sum |
sum := 0.
...sum...
```

you cannot possibly be confused about its type. Even if a temporary variable is initialized by a expression, you will be able to understand its type as long as the expression is well written:

```
| bounds |
bounds := self bounds.
... bounds ...
```

Role, on the other hand, requires explicit communication. You have probably had the experience of reading code whose temporary variables had names like "a," "b," and the ever popular "temp." As a reader, you have to go through the code holding these useless names in your head until the light comes on. "A ha! 'b' is really the left offset of the parent widget."

- *Name a temporary variable for the role it plays in the computation.*

Use variable naming as an opportunity to communicate valuable tactical information to future readers.

"results" is a good name for a Collecting Temporary Variable. "right" and "bottom" are good names for Explaining Temporary Variables.

Chapter

5

Collections

The collection hierarchy is one of the great strengths of Smalltalk. Code that has to be tediously written over and over in other languages is a single word in Smalltalk. The result is more flexible, because the collections respond to much of the same protocol, so a linear list can be converted to a hash table by substituting "Set" for "OrderedCollection."

The bad news is, the collection classes give you yet more stuff to learn so you can master Smalltalk. The good news is, no single piece of the protocol is complicated or hard to learn and the result is code that is simpler, faster, easier to maintain, and more flexible.

The very richness of the collection classes is their biggest drawback. Beginning programmers typically learn to use a small fraction of the available classes and messages, relying on leftover skills from procedural programming for the rest of the functionality they need. As a result, their code is much larger than it needs to be, difficult to read for an experienced Smalltalker, and more prone to error.

For example, it is common to find hand coded loops for iteration in beginner Smalltalk code. Not only is:

```
| index |
index := 1.
[index <= aCollection size] whileTrue:
     [...aCollection at: index...
     index := index + 1]
```

more difficult to write and read than:

```
aCollection do: [:each | ...each...]
```

it is also less flexible. The first code will only work with indexed collections. The second will work with Sets and Dictionaries, too.

During code reviews, I commonly find opportunities to transform four, five, or six line expressions into a single line using the full power of the collection protocol.

Our discussion of collections is divided into three sections:

*   Classes —When you want to use a collection, the first thing you have to decide is "which one." This section describes what problem or problems each of the major collection classes solve.

*   Protocol—Programming habits carried over from other languages can reduce the effectiveness of code when you use collections. This section describes the major messages you can send to collections and what problem each solves.

*   Idioms—Because collections are so powerful, there are a small set of standard tricks that experienced Smalltalkers know to play with them. If you are reading code that uses one of these idioms, you may be puzzled at first. This section introduces the problems you can solve using collections in unusual ways.

Classes

This section presents the circumstances under which you would choose to use each of the major collection classes.

Collection

- How do you represent a one-to-many relationship?

Every programming language provides facilities to represent one-to-many relationships. The first data structure in FORTRAN was the array.

Computer science has made a franchise of representing one-to-many relationships. How many thousands of varieties of trees, lists, and tables are there hidden away in the Journals of the ACM?

Such an important topic has picked up a vast quantity of idiom in every programming language. Even though I hardly use C any more, I can instantly recognize:

```
for (i = 0; i < n; i++) ...
```

as iterating over an array.

One of the most brilliant early developments in Smalltalk was presenting a unified protocol to all the varieties of ways of representing one-to-many relationships. No longer does all client code directly encode how to iterate over elements. Iteration is the responsibility of the object representing the relationship itself. This results in tremendous power throughout development. You can change from a linear list to a hash table by changing "OrderedCollection" to "Set," with the confidence that no other code will be affected.

The down side of the Collection classes is their very power. Because you can write code involving Collections in very few words, you have to be initiated in the special meaning of those words before you have a chance of understanding such code. Once you understand the vocabulary, though, you will never be able to write code in a language that doesn't support Collections without a wistful sigh about "how easy this would be in Smalltalk."

There is an alternative to using the Collection classes. Any class can be made indexable, that is have both named variables and variables you access through at: and at:put:. Using this feature, any class can be made to act like both a regular object and a collection, at the same time. This would be useful if you were extremely tight on space, but copying the Collection code just isn't worth it.

- *Use a Collection.*

A Library could keep a Collection of Books.

Use an OrderedCollection for Collections (p. 116) that change size dynamically. Use an Array (p. 133) for fixed-sized Collections. Use a Set (p. 119) to ensure element uniqueness. Use a Dictionary (p. 128) to map from one kind of object to another. Use a Temporarily Sorted Collection (p. 155) for ordering elements. Use a SortedCollection (p. 131) to keep elements in a computed order.

OrderedCollection

You need a dynamically sized Collection (p. 115).

- How do you code Collections whose size can't be determined when they are created?

Many of the hassles programs give users come from the need for flexibility. Primitive memory management has lead to a lack of flexibility in the sizes of data. Every time I read, "You can have up to 99 files" or "Each function can have no more than 256 lines," I imagine a software engineer preallocating memory to handle just that many items. While arbitrary limits like "99" or "256" are typically chosen because the engineers can't imagine the need for any more, just as typically, they become a hindrance to a user somewhere down the road (sometimes years down the road).

There is no excuse for arbitrary data size limitations in Smalltalk. Two factors work in your favor as you try to eliminate such limits. First, the Collection classes give you tremendous leverage to change your mind about representing one-to-many relationships. Second, the garbage collector frees you from the drudgery of maintaining references as data structures change size.

This flexibility comes at a cost. The implementation of OrderedCollection, the most common dynamically sized Collection, allocates more memory than it strictly needs at first, so that some growth can be accommodated at little cost. The implementation also uses indirection to access elements. In some Collection-intensive code, I have found this to be a bottleneck. While you're just trying to get the program working, though, you shouldn't worry about such issues. There is time enough to address them later.

- *Use an OrderedCollection as your default dynamically sized Collection.*

Here is an example of using OrderedCollection:

```
Class: Document
      superclass: Object
      instance variables: paragraphs
```

A Document stores an OrderedCollection of Paragraphs, defined here with Lazy Initialization:

```
Document>>paragraphs
      paragraphs isNil ifTrue: [paragraphs :=
OrderedCollection new].
      ^paragraphs
```

We need to be able to add new Paragraphs dynamically, so we need OrderedCollection's ability to change its size dynamically:

```
Document>>addParagraph: aParagraph
      self paragraphs add: aParagraph
```

Typesetting a Document is implemented by typesetting each Paragraph in turn. The order of the Paragraphs is important, so storing them in an OrderedCollection is exactly right.

```
Document>>typesetOn: aPrinter
      self paragraphs do: [:each | each typesetOn: aPrinter]
```

FORWARD

Change to a Set (p. 119) if you need to ensure that every element appears only once. Change to a RunArray (p. 118) if you want to compactly represent a collection with long runs of the same element. Change to an Array (p. 133) if you don't need dynamic sizing.

BACK

RunArray

You are using an OrderedCollection (p. 116).

- How do you compactly code an OrderedCollection or Array where you have the same element many times in a row?

The simplest solution is just to use an OrderedCollection. During early development, this is probably the right answer. When you begin working with realistic sized data sets, you may discover that you are using more memory than you can afford.

The classic example of this is text editing. Conceptually, each character in an editor has its own font, size, and decoration. The obvious representation of this is as an OrderedCollection of Style objects that parallels the characters. This might even work for short text. When you are dealing with a whole book, though, the extra four bytes for the slot in the OrderedCollection plus the 12 bytes for the Style header plus the 12 bytes for the variables in the Style plus all the bytes for the Font, Size, and Decoration objects really add up.

If you look at typical text, you'll see that most of the information is redundant. There will be 50 characters with one style, 200 with another, 90 with another, and so on. A RunArray stores this as "50 of style 1, 200 of style 2, 90 of style 3." Each count-object pair is called a "run."

If we stored this information in an OrderedCollection, we would need 340 elements. A RunArray needs only three runs (each with two references).

Storage efficiency comes at a cost. First, if you really have a different object in each element, a RunArray will take twice as much storage as an Array or OrderedCollection. Second, the time necessary to access an element at the end of a RunArray is proportional to the number of runs. The VisualWorks implementation avoids some of this cost by caching the position of the last element fetched.

- *Use a RunArray to compress long runs of the same element.*

A common example of using a RunArray is storing the emphasis for text. In a piece of text like this:

this **is a** test

the characters themselves can be stored in a 14 element String. The emphasis can be stored in a parallel 14 element array:

> #(plain plain plain plain plain bold bold bold bold plain plain plain plain plain)

This takes an extra four bytes per character, or 56 bytes. However, because there are so many adjacent elements that are the same, a RunArray can save space. You can think of it as storing:

> 5—#plain, 4—#bold, 5—#plain

This takes only 6 × 4 bytes, equaling 24 bytes.

I know I need a RunArray when I click "self" in an inspector of an Array or OrderedCollection and I see the same element printing over and over.

The beauty of using a RunArray is that client code can't know whether they have an Array, an OrderedCollection, or a RunArray, since they all support the same messages. You can code with whichever one works best, then change your mind later without any appreciable cost.

VisualWorks 2 implements RunArray. VisualAge and VisualSmalltalk do not at this writing.

Set

You need a Collection (p. 115) with unique elements. You may need a Collecting Parameter (p. 75) without duplicates. You may have been using an OrderedCollection (p. 116).

- How do you code a Collection whose elements are unique?

Suppose you have a Collection of Accounts and you want to send statements to all of the Owners. You don't have an explicit Collection of the Owners anywhere. You only want to send a single statement to each Owner. Each Owner could have a number of different Accounts.

How can we get each Owner only once? The naive code doesn't work right:

```
owners
    | results |
    results := OrderedCollection new.
    self accounts do: [:each | results add: each owner].
    ^results
```

We may get multiple copies of an Owner. You could solve this problem yourself by checking whether an owner was in the results before adding it:

```
owners
    | results |
    results := OrderedCollection new.
    self accounts do:
        [:each || owner |
        owner := each owner.
        (results includes: owner) ifFalse: [results add:
owner]].
    ^results
```

Sets solve this problem for you by ignoring "add: anObject" if anObject is already part of the Set. Using a Set instead of an OrderedCollection fixes the problem.

```
owners
    | results |
    results := Set new.
    self accounts do: [:each | results add: each owner].
    ^results
```

Another way of looking at the difference is by trying both Collections out in a workspace:

```
| o |
o := OrderedCollection new.
```

Put the String 'abc' in the Collection and it occurs once:

```
o add: 'abc'.
o occurrencesOf: 'abc' => 1
```

Put it in again, and it occurs twice:

```
o add: 'abc'.
o occurrencesOf: 'abc' => 2
```

Take it out once, and it only occurs once:

```
o remove: 'abc'.
o occurrencesOf: 'abc" => 1
```

Sets show different behavior.

```
| s |
s := Set new.
```

Like an OrderedCollection, put 'abc' in once and it occurs once:

```
s add: 'abc'.
s occurrencesOf: 'abc" => 1
```

But, put it in again, and it still only occurs once:

```
s add: 'abc'.
s occurrencesOf: 'abc" => 1
```

Take it out, and it's gone:

```
s remove: 'abc'.
s occurrencesOf: 'abc" => 0
```

(By the way, any time I'm trying to understand some new code, I pull out a workspace and start fiddling like this. There is no better way to understand a new object than to grab an instance and start sending it messages. If you think you know what's going on, try to predict how it will react. If you haven't a clue, just start sending messages and see what comes back.)

The elimination of duplicates comes at a cost. The order of adding and deleting that OrderedCollection preserves is not available for Sets. Also, OrderedCollection responds to the indexed messages at: and at: put:. Sets do not.

- *Use a Set.*

Use Sets when you don't want duplicates. If we want to get a Collection of all the members of all the clubs, we could just write:

```
clubMembers
        | results |
        results := OrderedCollection new.
        self clubs do: [:each | results addAll: each members].
        ^results
```

If one student could be in more than one club, that student would show up more than once in the result. To avoid this, we write:

```
clubMembers
        | results |
        results := Set new.
        self clubs do: [:each | results addAll: each members].
        ^results
```

Sets probably cause me the most incompatibility problems of any of the Collection classes. I am forever passing a Set to a list pane that expects an indexable Collection. It is easy enough to solve the problem by creating an Array or SortedCollection.

```
memberList: aPane
        aPane contents: self clubMembers
```

becomes:

```
memberList: aPane
    aPane contents: self clubMembers
asSortedCollection
```

Sets perform an important communication function. They are your way of telling your reader "I expect duplicates in this Collection, but I don't want them for further processing." Be sure you only use them when that is what you mean because that's how others will read your code.

The other reason to use a Set is because its implementation of includes: is much faster than the implementation in OrderedCollection (for large Collections). I have only done this a couple of times in my career, but it is a great trick to pull out when you're tuning performance.

If you implement an Equality Method (p. 124) for Set elements, you must also implement a Hashing Method (p. 126). You may need to convert to an Array (p. 133) or Temporarily Sorted Collection (p. 155) for clients who want an indexable Collection.

Equality Method

- How do you code equality for new objects?

The message "="is sent 1363 times in the standard VisualWorks 2 image. It is implemented 57 times. Clearly, this is a message of considerable importance.

The default implementation of equality is identity. Two objects are equal if, and only if, they are the same object.

```
Object>>= anObject
    ^self == anObject
```

If equality is only redefined 57 times, this definition must be good enough for the vast majority of classes.

The most important reason for implementing equality is because you are going to put your objects in a Collection and you want to be able to test for inclusion, remove elements, or eliminate duplicates in Sets without having to have the same instance.

For example, let's say I'm working on a library program. Two books are equal if the author and title are equal:

```
Book>>= aBook
        ^self author = aBook author & (self title = aBook title)
```

A Library maintains an OrderedCollection of Books. Because I have defined equality, I can write a method that takes the name of an author and a title and searches for that Book:

```
Library>>hasAuthor: authorString title: titleString
        | book |
        book := Book
                author: authorString
                title: titleString.
        ^self books includes: book
```

The other major reason to implement equality is because your objects have to interoperate with other objects that implement equality. For example, if I was implementing a new kind of Number, I would define equality because all Numbers define equality.

You see a fair number of class tests in equality methods. For example, you might see:

```
Book>>= aBook
    (aBook isMemberOf: self class) ifFalse: [^false].
    ^self author = aBook author & (self title = aBook title)
```

I read this as "If aBook isn't a Book, I couldn't possibly be equal to it. Otherwise, I'm equal if my author and title are equal to aBook's." While class tests are in general a bad thing (see Choosing Message), this is one place where they can be useful. What if we want to add Videos to our Library? Videos don't have a message "author," so comparing a Book and a Video without some protection would result in an error.

- *If you will be putting objects in a Set, using them as Dictionary keys, or otherwise using them with other objects that define equality, define a method called "=." Protect the implementation of "=" so only objects of compatible classes will be fully tested for equality.*

Value-like objects, like Numbers and Points, are the most obvious candidates for Equality Methods. Two Points are equal if their coordinates are equal.

```
Point>>= aPoint
    (aPoint isMemberOf: self class) ifFalse: [^false].
    ^x = aPoint x & (y = aPoint y)
```

You may need Double Dispatch (p. 55) for complex multiclass equality tests. Testing is often done in terms of Simple Delegation (p. 65) with one or more components of an object.

Hashing Method

You have written an Equality Method (p. 124). You may be putting new objects into a Set (p. 119). You may be using a new object as a key in a Dictionary (p. 128).

• How do you ensure that new objects work correctly with hashed Collections?

Once you understand the idea that you can override "=," the world becomes your oyster. New objects that have their own definition of equality automatically begin to play nicely with the rest of Smalltalk—almost.

Collection>>includes: uses equality:

```
Collection>>includes: anObject
    self do: [:each | each = anObject ifTrue: [^true]].
    ^false
```

So, you start out with an OrderedCollection and your newly equal objects and everything works fine. Then, you decide you need a Set. All of a sudden, you start getting bugs. You look at a Set and it has two objects in it that you know are equal. Weren't Sets supposed to avoid that problem?

The problem is that Set>>includes: doesn't just send "=," it also sends "hash." If two objects are equal but they don't return the same hash value, the Set is likely to miss the fact that they are equal.

• *If you override "=" and use the object with a hashed Collection, override "hash" so that two objects that are equal return the same hash value.*

This rule may seem kind of abstract. In practice, though, it is simple to satisfy this constraint. The Equality Method typically relies on some set of messages returning results that are equal:

```
Book>>= aBook
    ^self title = aBook title & (self author = aBook author)
```

My first cut implementation of "hash" is to get the hash values of all the messages that the Equality Method relies on and put them together with bit-wise exclusive-or.

Book>>hash
        ^self title hash bitXor: self author hash

This works whether the messages return Strings, Numbers, Arrays, or whatnot, because all the sub-components obey the Hashing Method pattern.

Hashing is often implemented in terms of Simple Delegation (p. 65).

Dictionary

You need a Collection (p. 115) that is indexed by something other than consecutive integers.

●   How do you map one kind of object to another?

Arrays and OrderedCollections map integers into objects. The integers must be between one and the size of the collection. Dictionaries are more flexible maps. Their keys may be any objects, instead of having to be sequential integers.

A typical use of a Dictionary is to map the names of things to the things:

```
colors
     | result |
     result := Dictionary new.
     result
          at: 'red'
          put: (Color red: 1).
     result
          at: 'gray'
          put: (Color brightness: 0.5).
     ^result
```

Another way to solve this problem is to add a "name" instance variable to Color. In fact, this seems to me the more "object-oriented" solution. Why doesn't this work?

Different parts of the system will want different names for the same color. A color called "red" in one place will be called "warning" in another. I suppose you could add a "colorName" and a "purposeName" instance variable to Color. Where would this end? Every new application of color would have to add a new instance variable. It is much easier to use a Dictionary in each object that needs a unique name.

Another way to solve this problem is to create an object that wraps a Color and gives it a name.

```
NamedColor
      superclass: Object
      instance variables: name color
```

Whenever I have implemented an object like this, it never gains any more responsibility than Getting Methods for the name and the wrapped object. It isn't worth it to create a new object just to do that. Associating a name with a color using a Dictionary only takes a few lines and is easily understood.

●   *Use a Dictionary.*

A common use for Dictionaries is giving names to things. For example, if I have a widget and different colors have different meanings, I might store them in a Dictionary:

```
Widget>>defaultColors
      | results |
      results := Dictionary new.
      results
            at: 'foreground'
            put: Color black.
      results
            at: 'background'
            put: Color mauve.
      ^results
```

Sometimes, programmers in a hurry use Dictionaries as cheap data structures. You can always spot code like this because two or more methods will use exactly the same fixed set of keys.

```
vitalInformation
    | result |
    result := Dictionary new.
    result
            at: 'weight'
            put: 190.
    result
            at: 'hair'
            put: 'blond'.
    ^result
checkOut: aPerson
    | info |
    info := aPerson vitalInformation.
    (info at: 'weight') < 280 & ((info at: 'hair') = 'black')
ifTrue: ...
```

I've also done the same thing with Arrays of fixed size where different indexes mean different things:

```
vitalInformation
    ^Array
            with: 190
            with: 'blond'
checkOut: aPerson
    | info |
    info := aPerson vitalInformation.
    (info at: 1) < 280 & ((info at: 2) = 'black') ifTrue: ...
```

This is your program's way of telling you "There's a new object here." The new object will have one instance variable for each element in the collection.

If you implement an Equality Method (p. 124) for Dictionary keys, you must also implement a Hashing Method (p. 126).

SortedCollection

You have a Collection (p. 115) that needs to be ordered according to some attributes of the elements.

- How do you sort a collection?

When I was in college, sorting was a big deal. I studied Knuth. I learned a dozen clever ways to sort. I listened to all the stories about how much computing time went into sorting algorithms and what an amazing impact even small improvements could have.

Imagine my distress when, after eleven years of Smalltalk programming, I have yet to write a sorting algorithm. All those brain cells wasted!

Not wasted, of course. To be an accomplished programmer you have to know what's going on under the hood. It's just that Smalltalk's collection classes turn awareness of how sorting is implemented into a rare and spectacular event.

Just as you have collections whose order is determined by when elements were added (OrderedCollection) and unordered but efficient (Set), sorting is just another attribute of a special kind of collection, SortedCollection.

- *Use a SortedCollection. Set its sort block if you want to sort by some criteria other than "<=."*

Any collection can be sorted by sending it "asSortedCollection."

By default, SortedCollections use "<" to compare elements. Numbers, Strings, Date and Time, and a few other objects already define "<." You will have to define "<" for your objects if you intend to put them in the result of "SortedCollection new."

SortedCollections internally use a two argument block to compare elements. You can set this sort block to anything you want. I could sort my children by age:

```
childrenByAge
        ^self children asSortedCollection: [:a :b | a age < b age]
```

because ages are Numbers and numbers define "<." I could just as easily sort them alphabetically by name:

```
children byName
        ^self children asSortedCollection: [:a :b | a name < b
name]
```

If you already have a SortedCollection and you want to change its order, you can send it "sortBlock: aBlock" to change the order.

```
self childrenByAge sortBlock: [:a :b | a income > b income]
```

One performance nasty to look out for is if you build a SortedCollection one element at a time. SortedCollections re-sort every time an element is added or deleted. If you need to build a SortedCollection an element at a time, consider using an OrderedCollection temporarily, then turning it into a SortedCollection when it is complete.

Array

BACK

You need a Collection (p. 115) with a fixed number of elements. You may have been using an OrderedCollection (p. 116).

- How do you code a collection with a fixed number of elements?

OrderedCollection extols the virtues of flexibility. How many elements do you need? Why decide now? Just use an OrderedCollection and avoid any arbitrary limits.

What if you know when you create it exactly how big a collection will be? You could use an OrderedCollection and add elements, but the code would have lost the information that the size of the collection is fixed. Your code will communicate better if you say, "Here's a collection. Here's how big it is. That won't ever change."

The second reason to use a fixed size collection is efficiency. The flexibility of an OrderedCollection comes at the cost of an extra message to access elements. Most implementations also split OrderedCollections into two objects, so there is extra space overhead as well.

Usually, you don't care about the efficiency, but I did one performance tuning gig where I got a 40 percent speed-up by replacing the OrderedCollections with Arrays. Of course, the code looked like FORTRAN, not Smalltalk, but when you're tuning performance you're not out to save the world, just make it go a little faster.

- *Use an Array. Create it with "new: anInteger" so that it has space for the number of elements you know it needs.*

Ward Cunningham taught me the trick of simulating variable sized arrays. It is only valid if you are accessing the Array much more than you are adding to it and removing from it. Code that reads:

```
children := OrderedCollection new
```

you change into:

```
children := Array new "or even #()"
```

When you need to add an element, Instead of adding it to the collection:

```
children add: anObject
```

you create a new Array with the element added and assign it to the variable:

```
children := children copyWith: anObject
```

Similarly, for removing elements:

```
children remove: anObject
```

you create a new Array without the element:

```
children := children copyWithout: anObject
```

FORWARD

Use a ByteArray (p. 135) to store SmallIntegers in the range 0..255. Use an Interval (p. 137) to represent an Array of sequential Numbers. Use a RunArray (p. 118) to compactly store Arrays that have long runs of repeated elements.

ByteArray

BACK

You need to represent an Array (p. 133) of small numbers.

- How do you code an Array of numbers in the range 0..255 or -128..127?

Software engineering was born in a resource starved environment. There have never been enough cycles or enough memory to do what we want. While this was more true in the past than it is today, the increasing demands of application consumers will always push the available resources.

One of the most creative reactions to the lack of available memory has been the ways software engineering has found to use eight bit bytes. The EBCDIC and ASCII codes encode printable characters as bytes. The P-Code and Smalltalk byte code instruction sets encode virtual machine instructions as bytes. The concatenation of four or eight bytes can form a memory address.

On the one hand, you would like your Smalltalk program to be as insulated as possible from representation decisions, in order to be as flexible as possible. On the other hand, some consideration of space efficiency must be possible so you can code in a still finite environment.

There are times when you really mean to communicate that information is stored as eight bit bytes. Then, using a more general representation would actually be misleading. You want to use the representation that most directly communicates your intent.

The collection classes provide an excellent means for achieving the flexibility of a hidden representation and the space efficiency of encoding information as bytes. Choosing a representation that stores only bytes effectively communicates that the objects contained in that collection can only be SmallIntegers in the range 0..255.

- *Use a ByteArray.*

ByteArrays are used to store homogenous information, like the pixels in an image or the floating point numbers in a vector.

```
Class: Vector
     superclass: Object
     instance variables: numbers
```

When you create a Vector of a certain size, it allocates enough bytes to store that many Floats:

```
Vector class>>new: anInteger
     ^self new setNumbers: (ByteArray new: anInteger * 4)
Vector>>setNumbers: aByteArray
     numbers := aByteArray
```

Setting an element in a Vector takes the bytes out of the Float and puts them into the ByteArray:

```
Vector>>at: anInteger put: aFloat
     1 to: 4 do:
          [:each |
          numbers
               at: anInteger * 4 + each + 1
               put: (aFloat basicAt: each)]
```

When SmallIntegers are in a ByteArray, they are represented much as you would represent them in C or assembly language—simple eight bit patterns. The code for at:put: converts from Smalltalk's format for SmallIntegers into eight bit patterns. The code for at: does the reverse conversion.

If you are storing lots of information as bytes, you may find dramatic increases in speed or decreases in memory footprint after changing a few references to "Array" into references to "ByteArray." For current Smalltalk systems with 32-bit object references, the savings is a factor of four. If you have lots of small ByteArrays, don't expect the same savings because the space overhead of each ByteArray (typically 8 or 12 bytes) will be large compared to the information stored in it.

Interval

● How do you code a collection of numbers in sequence?

Every once in a while, you will find yourself writing code to create an Array and initialize its elements to sequential numbers:

```
| indexes |
indexes := Array new: 100.
1 to: indexes size do:
    [:each |
    indexes
        at: each
        put: each]
```

This is not a very direct way to communicate "an Array of sequential numbers." Also, it takes space and time to represent an Array of numbers like this.

There is a special collection class called Interval that is built expressly for this purpose. There is really no down side to using Interval. Your code will read better and be faster.

● *Use an Interval with start, stop, and an optional step value. The Shortcut Constructor Methods Number>>to: and to:by: build Intervals for you.*

Some of the code you write using Intervals can be confusing at first.

```
1 to: 20 do: [:each | ...]
```

is equivalent to:

```
(1 to: 20) do: [:each | ...]
```

Even though the two phrases look similar, very different code is being invoked. In the first case, the message to:do: is being sent to the SmallInteger 1. In the second, the message to: is being sent to the SmallInteger 1. This returns an Interval that is then sent the message do:.

You can translate prose descriptions of number sequences into Intervals:

Description	Interval
One to ten	1 to: 10
Even numbers from zero to fifty	0 to: 50 by: 2
Count down from 99 ?by threes	99 to: 0 by: -3

There are some enumerations you'd like to do that aren't supported by the enumeration protocol. For example, although there is a Number>>to:do:, there isn't a Number>>to:collect:. However, you can use an Interval because it is a full fledged collection.

For example, if I have an Array and I want an Array of Associations, the keys of which are the indexes of the original Array and the values of which are the elements, I can write:

```
(1 to: anArray size) collect:
        [:each |
        Association
              key: each
              value: (anArray at: each)]
```

Collection Protocol

The uniform protocol of the collection classes are one of their greatest strengths. Client code is effectively decoupled from decisions about how to store a collection by using a common set of messages.

Many Smalltalk programmers take a long time to learn all the collection protocol. They begin with a couple of messages, like do:, add:, and size, and then stick with them for a long time.

When I started programming in Smalltalk, I can remember being overwhelmed by it. There is a lot to learn just to achieve basic competence. However, the collection protocol is one of the highest leverage pieces of the system. The better you can use it, the faster you can code and the faster you can read other folks' code.

This section highlights the most important messages in the collection repertoire. It is by no means exhaustive. I selected these messages to pattern because they are the ones I see most often missed or misused.

After you master these messages, take a day or so to make a thorough study of which messages are available in which collection classes. In no time, you'll be coding collections like a pro.

IsEmpty

- How do you test if a collection is empty?

I wouldn't have thought I'd have to point this one out, but over and over I see code that says:

```
...aCollection size = 0 ifTrue: ...
```

or

```
...aCollection size > 0 ifTrue: ...
```

Checking whether size is equal to zero or greater than zero is really an implementation of a higher level concept, namely "Is the collection empty?"

The collection protocol provides simple messages that test collections for emptiness. Using them results in more readable code.

- *Send isEmpty to test whether a collection is empty (has no elements). Use notEmpty to test whether a collection has elements.*

All the Smalltalks have a simple facility for popping up a dialog that asks the user to type in an answer. A blank answer indicates that the operation shouldn't proceed. The following code (VisualWorks style) is common:

```
| answer |
answer := Dialog request: 'Number, please?'.
answer isEmpty ifTrue: [^self].
...
```

Note that while VisualSmalltalk and VisualAge also define notEmpty, VisualWorks 2 does not, so you'll have to add it yourself.

The value of isEmpty is not that there is such a huge difference between:

```
aCollection size = 0
```

and:

```
    aCollection isEmpty
```

although there is some difference. The important point is that I can read the idiomatic version instantly. If I see some code explicitly checking the size, I have to stop and figure out if there is something special going on that isn't obvious.

All cultures develop their own vocabulary. If you were in a repair shop and you heard someone say, "hand me that wrench with the knurled wheel that changes the width," you wouldn't want them working on your car. You want a mechanic who knows it's a monkey wrench.

Includes:

- How do you search for a particular element in a collection?

Many people's first instinct is to use the enumeration protocol to implement searching. They will write code like this:

```
| found |
found := false.
aCollection do: [:each | each = anObject ifTrue: [found :=
true]].
...
```

With more experience, you might see a more sophisticated enumeration message:

```
| found |
found := (aCollection
        detect: [:each | each = anObject]
        ifNone: [nil]) notNil.
...
```

The collection protocol provides you with a message to do exactly this, includes:.

The above code would look like this using includes:

```
| found |
found := aCollection includes: anObject
...
```

You could probably even eliminate the temporary variable and just use the expression in line.

Importantly, includes: is available to be optimized. Some kinds of collections, like Set, execute it in constant time, independent of the size of the collection. The alternatives to includes:, above, will always take time proportional to the size of the collection.

- *Send includes: and pass the object to be searched for.*

An example from Collection Accessor Method returns true if the receiver employs a person:

```
employs: aPerson
        ^employees includes aPerson
```

A common use of includes is to compute the intersection of two collections:

collection1 select: [:each | collection2 includes: each]

You will have to implement an Equality Method (p. 124) and a Hashing Method (p. 126) for your own objects, if you want to search based on contents instead of identity.

Concatentation

● How do you put two collections together?

Concatentation is one of those intermediate idioms in most languages. You can get along without it but pretty soon you have to learn how. The typical concatenation idiom goes something like this:

1. Create a collection big enough for the result.
2. Copy the first collection into the first part of the result.
3. Copy the second collection into the second part of the result.

Sometimes, there is a library function to do both copies for you.

Smalltalk simplifies this to a single message you send to the first collection, "," (comma), with the second collection as an argument.

Many programming languages treat strings specially. Often, the "+" (plus) operator is used for string concatenation. In Smalltalk, Strings are just collections of characters. All the usual collection protocol works. In particular, to concatenate strings, you use "," just as you would if you were dealing with Arrays or OrderedCollections.

Concatenate two collections by sending "," to the first with the second as an argument.

Concatentation is often used when constructing messages from a String and some arguments:

> self error: anInteger printString , ' is too many objects for ' , aString

You may need a Concatenating Stream (p. 165) if you are putting together lots of collections.

Enumeration

- How do you execute code across a collection?

Once you have a collection, you have to do something with it. Examples of computations across collections are:

- An Account computes its balance by totaling up the values of all of its Transactions.
- A composite Visual displays by displaying all of its components.
- Deleting a Directory deletes all of its Files.

Procedural programmers develop a toolbox of idioms for writing code like this. Ask a C programmer to iterate over an array, and chances are they will be able to program as fast as they can type. Visual recognition of such code becomes automatic, also.

Smalltalk hides the details of iteration behind a set of uniform messages that all collections understand. Rather than have one, two, or three line idioms, Smalltalk uses single word messages. Code written using these messages is easy to write correctly and easy to read correctly.

Because there are several variations on the enumeration messages, some Smalltalk programmers learn one or two and code the rest by hand. In the end, it takes longer to write code that is bigger, more error prone, and harder to read than if they just used the messages that are there.

- *Use the enumeration messages to spread a computation across a collection.*

Enumeration messages work fine for empty collections. You can use this to avoid special case code for the case that a collection is empty.

```
printChildren
        children isEmpty ifTrue: [^self].
        self children do: [:each | each print]
```

is exactly the same as:

```
printChildren
        self children do: [:each | each print]
```

You will have problems if you are iterating over a Collection at the same time you are adding or removing elements:

```
aSet do: [:each | aSet remove: each]
```

There isn't often a call to write this kind of code. If you must, make a copy of the collection to enumerate:

```
aSet copy do: [:each | aSet remove each]
```

FORWARD *Use Do (p. 146) for simple enumeration. Use Collect (p. 147) to transform the elements of a collection. Use Select/Reject (p. 149) to select only certain portions of a collection. Use Detect (p. 151) to search for an element. Use Inject:Into: (p. 152) to keep a running total across a collection.*

Do

- How do you execute code for each element in a collection?

This is the fundamental message out of which the rest of the enumeration messages are built. If this were a procedural language, you would have a small set of idioms for iterating through a collection, one for a linked list, one for an array, one for a hash table.

For purposes of enumeration, there is no difference between the collection classes in Smalltalk. As a programmer, you never explicitly deal with walking pointers along a list or iterating a loop counter. You just send the message "do:" and magic happens.

In spite of the simplicity of do:, I still occasionally see code where someone slips into previous habits and writes:

```
index := 1.
[index <= aCollection size] whileTrue:
        [...aCollection at: index...
        index := index + 1]
```

There is really no excuse for this. The code using do: is much shorter and easier to read:

```
aCollection do: [:each | ...each...]
```

There is a small performance difference between the two. I measured open coded iteration on VisualSmalltalk for Windows 3.0.1 at 1 millisecond for a thousand element Array, while sending do: took 1.7 milliseconds. If you are doing any processing at all on the elements, the loop overhead will immediately disappear, and if you have to go in later and open code a few iterations, it is no big deal.

- *Send do: to a collection to iterate over its elements. Send a one argument block as the argument to do:. It will be evaluated once for each element.*

Operations like Collection>>add: that are also defined for a Collection of parameters (Collection>>addAll:) are often implemented with do: and the simpler operation:

```
Collection>>addAll: aCollection
    aCollection do: [:each | self add: each]
```

I was raised on Pascal and C. I got good at writing loops, putting the index increments in just the right place. After about six months of Smalltalk, though, I just couldn't seem to remember to manually update loop indexes when I had to write out an enumeration by hand. I would always forget to put the increment in, or I'd decrement instead of increment. It was embarrassing at times. I'm happy to say, I've mostly recovered since then, but it's kind of a nice skill to be able to lose.

Use a Simple Enumeration Parameter (p. 182) in the block.

Collect

- How do you operate on the result of a message sent to each object in the collection?

If this was good old procedural programming, we'd probably write code where the enumeration block sent a message to the element, then used the result of the message in further computation.

```
self children do: [:each | self passJudgement: each
    hairStyle]
```

Other code, that also wanted to deal with hair styles, would have similar code:

```
self children do: [:each | self trim: each hairStyle]
```

This violates the once and only once rule. The two code fragments look very similar except for the operation to be performed on the hair style.

We can capture the commonality of the code by creating an intermediate collection that contains the results of the messages sent to each element of the original collection. We can then enumerate over the new collection.

The new clarity of the code comes at the cost of creating a new collection to hold the transformed elements and iterating over the collection twice: once to transform it and once to compute with it. If you measure a performance problem coming from intermediate collections, it is easily fixed later. Better communication is definitely worth the cost, and chances are you'll never have a performance problem because of it.

● *Use collect: to create a new collection whose elements are the results of evaluating the block passed to collect: with each element of the original collection. Use the new collection.*

We can use Composed Method with collect: to capture the common part of the above code:

```
childrenHairStyles
    ^self children collect: [:each | each hairStyle]
```

Then we can simplify the code fragments:

```
self childrenHairStyles do: [:each | self passJudgement: each]
self childrenHairStyles do: [:each | self trim: each]
```

If you must, improve performance of code using collect: with a special Enumeration Method (p. 144). Use a Simple Enumeration Parameter (p. 182) in the block argument.

Select/Reject

- How do you filter out part of a collection?

The procedural solution is to have an enumeration block that does two things—test the element for "interesting-ness" and conditionally perform some action on the interesting ones. Code written in this style looks like this:

```
self children do: [:each | each isResponsible ifTrue: [self
buyCar: each]]
```

Code like this is fine the first time you write it, but chances are more than likely that you'll want the same filter somewhere else:

```
self children do: [:each | each isResponsible ifTrue: [self
addToWill: each]]
```

Remember the rule about saying things once and only once? These two pieces of code violate that rule. Everything up to that second square bracket is exactly the same. We'd like to capture that commonality, somehow.

The solution is to create a collection containing only interesting elements, then operating on that. The new collection comes at a cost—it has to be created separately from the original collection. What is an efficient garbage collector for, if not to let you make your code more expressive. If creating the intermediate collections is too expensive, you can easily fix them later.

- *Use select: and reject: to return new collections containing only elements of interest. Enumerate the new collection. Both take a one argument Block that returns a Boolean. Select: gives you ele-*

ments for which the Block returns true, reject: gives you elements for which the Block returns false.

To capture the commonality of the above two pieces of code, we use Composed Method with select: to create a method that returns responsible children:

```
responsibleChildren
        ^self children select: [:each | each isResponsible]
```

Then we can simplify the two code fragments:

```
self responsibleChildren do: [:each | self buyCar: each]
```

```
self responsibleChildren do: [:each | self addToWill: each]
```

FORWARD

You can use a special purpose Enumeration Method to avoid the cost of creation. Use a Simple Enumeration Parameter in the block argument. Use a Lookup Cache to optimize performance.

Detect

- How do you search a collection?

Another common collection idiom is searching for an element that meets certain criteria. Of course, you can implement this using do: , testing the criteria inside the enumeration block, and executing some code conditionally. This code gives the car keys to the first responsible child:

```
self children do: [:each | each isResponsible ifTrue: [each
giveKeys: self carKeys. ^self]]
```

Notice that you have to be sure to only execute the conditional code once. Managing this in a complex loop can result in code that is very hard to follow.

- *Search a collection by sending it detect:. The first element for which the block argument evaluates to true will be returned.*

Detect takes a one argument block as an argument, which should evaluate to true or false. It returns the first element for which the block evaluates to true. The code above turns into:

```
(self children detect: [:each | each isResponsible])
giveKeys: self carKeys
```

There is a variation of detect:, detect:ifNone:, that takes an additional zero parameter Block as an argument. Use this if you're not sure any element will be found.

Detect:ifNone: gives rise to a clever ("hard to read, at least at first") idiom. What if you want to return true from a method if any element meets a criterion and false otherwise?

```
hasResponsibleChild
    self children
        detect: [:each | each isResponsible]
        ifNone: [^false].
    ^true
```

I use this occasionally but I can't say I'm particularly proud of it.

Use a Simple Enumeration Parameter (p. 182) in the first block argument. Use a Lookup Cache (p. 161) to optimize performance.

Inject:into:

You need an Enumeration (p. 144) that keeps a running value.

- How do you keep a running value as you iterate over a Collection?

One of the first procedural programming patterns everyone learns is keeping a running total.

1. Initialize the total.

2. For each element of a collection, modify the total (sum, min, max, whatever).

3. Use the result.

Thus, you see a lot of Smalltalk code that looks like this:

```
| max |
max := 0.
self children do: [:each | max := max max: each value].
^max
```

This is so common, in fact, that there is a message that does it for you.

Why doesn't everybody use this mysterious and powerful message? Because it has a funky name. People see the name and they think, "No way can I figure out what that does. Better leave it alone." This is no excuse for not using it, though. When what you mean is "Keep a running value over this collection," you should use the message, strange name and all.

- *Use inject:into: to keep a running value. Make the first argument the initial value. Make the second argument a two element block. Call the block arguments "sum" and "each." Have the block evaluate to the next value of the running value.*

The code above becomes:

```
^self children
    inject: 0
    into: [:sum :each | sum max: each]
```

There is a clever use of inject:into: that I just learned. Usually, I use "clever" as an insult but I just can't help but show this one. The problem is iterating over adjacent pairs in a collection. That is, I want to evaluate some code for elements one and two, then elements two and three, and so on. Here's how you use inject:into: for this:

```
self children
    inject: nil
    into:
        [:eachPrevious :eachNext |
        eachPrevious notNil ifTrue: [...].
        eachNext]
```

The first time through the loop, eachPrevious is nil and eachNext is the first element of the collection. The conditional code isn't evaluated. The whole block evaluates to the first element of the collection. The second time through, eachPrevious is the first element of the collection and eachNext is the second element. The conditional code gets executed. This keeps going until eachPrevious is the second to last element and eachNext is the last element.

Collection Idioms

Once you are comfortable using the collection protocol, you can begin using collections to solve higher level tasks. Here are a few of the common ways collections are used.

BACK

Duplicate Removing Set

You have a Collection (p. 115).

- How do you remove the duplicates from a Collection?

I remember answering this question on a test in school. I know I've seen the C-ish code for it while reviewing code. It always looks ugly:

```
unique := OrderedCollection new.
self owners do: [:each | (unique includes: each) ifFalse:
[unique add: each]]
```

No need for that in Smalltalk. Once you get over the idea that allocating memory is expensive in programming or execution time, and once you get used to the power of the Collection classes, problems like this become trivial.

- *Send "asSet" to the Collection. The result will have all duplicates removed.*

If I want a Collection containing all my children with blue eyes or blond hair, where some children may have both, I can use this pattern.

```
| nordic |
nordic := (self blueEyedChildren , self
blondHairedChildren) asSet.
...
```

I sure wish I'd been using Smalltalk when I was in college!

When you tune performance, you may find that you are creating Collections for the same elements over and over and over. Composing all those intermediate Collections together is no big deal. Remember, you're going for clarity of expression.

Use a Temporarily Sorted Collection (p. 155) if you need the unique elements sorted.

FORWARD

BACK

Temporarily Sorted Collection

You have a Collection (p. 115). You may have implemented a Comparing Method (p. 32) but want to sort the objects differently.

- How do you present a Collection with one of many sort orders?

The obvious solution is to store the Collection as a SortedCollection in the first place. Every time you change the sort order, you can change the sort block of the SortedCollection.

If you wouldn't otherwise have to have the Collection sorted, this solution causes more problems than it solves. You may not want to pay the price of a SortedCollection most of the time. You may want several sort orders at the same time.

You can solve the problem by handing out copies of the Collection. Then you have the problem of coordinating additions and removals from the Collection. This problem is usually much less severe than trying to manage several sort orders with the same Collection.

- *Return a sorted copy of the Collection by sending "asSortedCollection" to the Collection. Send "asSortedCollection: aBlock" for custom sort orders.*

A common use for this pattern is presenting information in a list, especially if you have just used Duplicate Removing Set:

```
candidateList
    ^self candidates asSet asSortedCollection: [:a :b | a
name < b name]
```

Stack

• How do you implement a stack?

One of the first objects many people write when they come to Smalltalk is Stack. Stack is the basic data structure, fabled in song, story, and hundreds of papers about theoretical programming languages.

Algorithms that use stacks can be simply expressed in Smalltalk. The syntax lends itself to readable code written in terms of pushes and pops. However, there is no Stack class in any of the basic images. I've seen one written any number of times, but they never seem to last long. Smalltalk programmers need stacks, too. What do they do?

It's easy to simulate a stack using OrderedCollection:

Stack Operation	OrderedCollection message
push	addLast:
pop	removeLast:
top	last
depth	size
empty	isEmpty

The result doesn't read exactly like a stack would read, but the idiom is so recognizable that the cost of using the idiom is far less than the cost of adding a new class to the image.

Why doesn't this result in confusing code? Why don't you write part of the algorithm using an OrderedCollection as a stack, then forget and start using it as a queue?

If there is a part of the algorithm that is complicated, you make a method or an object that gives it a simple public face. When you ask of the result "How many methods know this OrderedCollection is really a stack?," the answer is typically one. You use a Role Suggesting Temporary Variable name to communicate that the OrderedCollection is being used as a stack. End of story.

Why is there no Stack in Smalltalk? Well, "just because." It is part of the culture to simulate stacks using OrderedCollection. If that's how everybody does it, and it doesn't cost you anything, that's how you do it, too.

• *Implement a Stack using an OrderedCollection.*

If your stack only needs to be used within a single method, you can store it in a temporary variable:

```
| tasks newTask nextTask |
...
...tasks addLast: newTask...
...
...nextTask := tasks removeLast...
...
```

If the whole object needs to share the stack, communicate the presence of the stack with Intention Revealing Messages:

```
pushTask: aTask
      tasks addLast: aTask
popTask
      ^tasks removeLast
```

You may need Composed Method (p. 21) to simplify code using OrderedCollections (p. 116) as Stacks, so the idiom is not confusing.

Queue

- How do you implement a queue?

The story for queues is much like the story for stacks. Everyone simulates them using OrderedCollections:

Queue Operation	OrderedCollection message
add	addFirst:
remove	removeLast:
empty	isEmpty
length	size

As with stacks, you lose a little by translating the queue operations into messages to OrderedCollection protocol, but not nearly enough to make up for the cost of adding a new class.

- *Implement queues using an OrderedCollection.*

I have used OrderedCollections as queues a couple of ways. The most common is in implementing level-order traversal, where you need to visit all the depth 1 nodes of a tree before you visit the depth 2 nodes and so on.

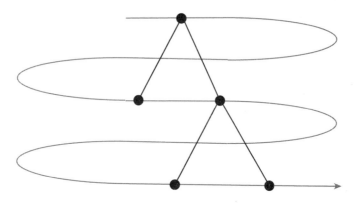

The code looks like this:

```
Node>>levelOrderDo: aBlock
    | queue |
    queue := OrderedCollection with: self.
    [queue isEmpty] whileFalse:
        [| current |
        current := queue removeLast.
        aBlock value: current.
        queue addAllFirst: current children]
```

You can implement a priority queue with a SortedCollection using add: and removeFirst:, instead of addFirst: and removeLast:.

> I can vividly remember the moment I became a computer scientist. I was in a first data structure class taught by Andrzej Proskurowski at the University of Oregon. Gray light through the windows washed most of the color out of the room (we are talking about Eugene, Oregon, here). I was just getting comfortable with data structures as a concept separate from programming but I was still squirming a bit sitting there, since Andrzej was a pretty aggressive professor.
>
> Andrzej had the size and energy of a hummingbird but was muscled like a gymnast. He had a thick black goatee and an even thicker Polish accent. He kept us all on our toes with the simple trick of calling everyone by name after hearing the names exactly once. He had just presented a linked list implementation of queues in Pascal using a header record. I followed pretty well, a first for me, when I got a conviction that there was a shorter implementation.
>
> I could see nothing but my notebook as I scrambled to code in my head, and then on paper, a version that used a footer record instead. Sure enough, I could slice one line out of one of the routines. After class, I hustled over to the computer center to try it out. Bingo! It ran. I rushed over to Andrzej's office to show him my gem. He was skeptical at first, but we went over it and he congratulated me on my success. It was the first time I'd spoken to a professor one on one. I was overwhelmed.
>
> I have since given up computer science for software engineering, but writing this has given me a renewed sense of how important that little bit of transformation was for me.

Searching Literal

- How do you search for one of a few literal objects known when you write the code?

If Smalltalk had a case statement, you would be tempted to write

```
Character>>isVowel
    case self asLowercase of
        $a:
        $e:
        $i:
        $o:
        $u: ^true
    otherwise: ^false
```

(I'm suggesting case statement syntax. A Choosing Message is almost always better than hard coded cases, anyway.)

Since Smalltalk doesn't have a case statement, you generally have to resort to Boolean or conditional logic:

```
Character>>isVowel
    | lower |
    lower := self asLowercase.
    ^lower = $a | (lower = $e) | (lower = $i) | (lower = $o) |
(lower = $u)
```

Pretty ugly, eh? Not as bad as:

```
Character>>isVowel
    self = $a | (self = $A) ifTrue: [^true].
    self = $e | (self = $E) ifTrue: [^true].
    self = $i | (self = $I) ifTrue: [^true].
    self = $o | (self = $O) ifTrue: [^true].
    self = $u | (self = $U) ifTrue: [^true].
    ^false
```

Because Strings are literals, you can use the collection protocol to implement the same thing much more compactly:

```
Character>>isVowel
        ^'aeiou' includes: self asLowercase
```

• *Ask a literal Collection if it includes the element you are seeking.*

You can do the same thing with Symbols:

```
Style>>isFancy: aSymbol
        ^#(bold italic) includes: aSymbol
```

This is not a trick that comes up every day, but used occasionally it can save you a few lines of code.

Lookup Cache

• *How do you optimize complex Detect or Select/Reject loops?*

The simplest solution is just to keep your code in its original form. Sometimes, what you are doing is looking up an element by a simple attribute:

```
childNamed: aString
        ^self children detect: [:each | each name = aString]
```

Sometimes, you are computing subsets of the elements in a collection:

```
childrenWithHairColor: aString
    ^self children select: [:each | each hairColor = aString]
```

These are simple to write and simple to read. This first time you need code like this, you should definitely write it in terms of Enumeration.

For large collections or frequently computed expressions, this kind of computation can be a performance bottleneck. If you measure a problem with one of these expressions, you may be able to cache the result of computation and reuse it rather than recomputing it.

As with all caches, you will only be able to do this if you can keep the contents of the cache synchronized with changes to the collection and its elements.

- *Prepend "lookup" to the name of the expensive search or filter method. Add an instance variable holding a Dictionary to cache results. Name the variable by appending "Cache" to the name of the search. Make the parameters of the search the keys of the Dictionary and the results of the search the values.*

The first example above turns into a variable called "nameCache." First, we change the original method to:

```
lookupChildNamed: aString
    ^self children detect: [:each | each name = aString]
```

Assuming the variable holding the lookup cache is initialized (see Explicit Initialization and Lazy Initialization), we rewrite "childNamed:" as:

```
childNamed: aString
    ^nameCache
        at: aString
        ifAbsentPut: [self lookupChildNamed: aString]
```

VisualWorks doesn't implement at:ifAbsentPut: and VisualAge takes an object as the second parameter, not a Block, so you have to write:

```
childNamed: aString
    ^nameCache
        at: aString
        ifAbsent:
            [nameCache
                at: aString
                put: (self lookupChildNamed: aString)]
```

The second example above has collections as the values in the Dictionary instead of single objects, but other than that, the pattern plays out similarly:

```
lookupChildrenWithHairColor: aString
    ^self children select: [:each | each hairColor = aString]
childrenWithHairColor: aString
    ^hairColorCache
        at: aString
        ifAbsentPut: [self lookupChildrenWithHairColor:
aString]
```

Parsing Stream

- How do you write a simple parser?

You will probably have to write simple parsers in Smalltalk. I don't mean the kind that computer scientists love, with lots of Ls and Rs and numbers in their name. I mean the simple kind, where each line has a keyword and then a bunch of information, different depending on the keyword.

One simple way to structure code like this is by grabbing a line at a time and parsing it.

```
parse: aStream
    [aStream atEnd] whileFalse: [self parseLine: aStream
nextLine]

parseLine: aString
    | reader |
    reader := ReadStream on: aString.
    keyword := reader nextWord.
    keyword = 'one' ifTrue: [self parseOne: reader].
    keyword = 'two' ifTrue: [self parseTwo: reader].
    ...
```

This leads to code that creates Strings and Streams all over the place. Something (a String or Stream) has to be passed to each method. If the methods are deeply nested, that extra parameter becomes tedious. It is error-prone, too, since it is easy to forget whether you are dealing with a String or a Stream.

In many cases, having many methods share the same instance variable is dangerous, especially if it is an object that will be side effected by many methods. A change in one method is likely to affect others inadvertently. In the case of parsing, though, the danger is minimized because of the simple nature of the control flow.

- *Put the Stream in an instance variable. Have all parsing methods work from the same Stream.*

Using this pattern, the code above looks like:

```
parse: aStream
        reader := aStream. "Reader is now an instance
variable."
        [reader atEnd] whileFalse: [self parseLine]

parseLine
        keyword := reader nextWord.
        keyword = 'one' ifTrue: [^self parseOne].
        keyword = 'two' ifTrue: [^self parseTwo].
        ...
```

The lack of parameters cleans up the code considerably. Each parsing method has to be careful to leave the Parsing Stream in a known state so the other methods can simply assume where they are in the String.

The "case statement," formed by the conditionals in parseLine above, leads some folks to want a "real" case statement in Smalltalk. For me, having to write the code above once a year just isn't sufficient justification for adding a new language feature.

Concatenating Stream

You may be collecting results in a Collecting Temporary Variable (p. 105). You may be collecting results over several methods in a Collecting Parameter (p. 75).

- How do you concatenate several Collections?

Concatenation is a simple way to join several Collections. When you have lots of Collections, though, it can be slow because the objects in the first Collection are copied once for each Collection that is concatenated.

Streams provide a way out of this dilemma. Streams are careful not to copy their contents many times, even as the Collection they are streaming over gets larger.

- *Use a Stream to concatenate many Collections.*

I ran a quick benchmark to see how significant the difference was between Collection concatenation and Streams. I ran the following code, which concatenates one thousand Strings:

```
100 timesRepeat:
    [result := String new.
    1000 timesRepeat: [result := result , 'abcdefg']]
```

It took 53 seconds to run. Then I ran the Stream version:

```
100 timesRepeat:
    [writer := WriteStream on: String new.
    1000 timesRepeat: [writer nextPutAll: 'abcdefg'].
    writer contents]]
```

It took 0.9 seconds to run. The difference is a factor of almost 60.

Sometimes, you will use Concatenating Stream not because it is your choice, but because you have to fit into other code that already uses it. The most common example is specializing object printing by overriding printOn:.

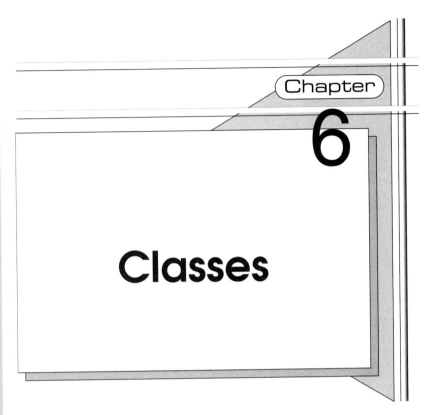

Classes

There is probably no coding decision with more effect on the quality of your code than names you give your classes. If computers were the only audience for code, we could just call them C1, C2, C3, and have done. The expensive reader is not the computer, it is other people.

Naming classes is your biggest billboard for communicating about your system. The first thing readers will look at when they look at your code is the names of the classes. Those names will go beyond your code. Insidiously, they leak into everyday conversation—and not just for developers. Ten years down the road, you will hear users who know nothing about programming using the class names you chose.

Good class names provide insight into the purpose and design of a system. They reveal underlying metaphors. They communicate themes and variations. They break the system into parts and show how the parts get put back together.

Great naming is an art and will always remain so (just ask Madison Avenue). Good naming is in the reach of everyone. Avoiding obvious mistakes and producing names that work together will boost your class names above average.

167

Simple Superclass Name

- What do you call a class that is expected to be the root of an inheritance hierarchy?

All naming decisions have several constraints in common. You want names that are as short as possible, so they are easy to type, format, and say. At the same time, you want to convey as much information as possible in each name, so readers will not have to carry as much knowledge in their heads. You want names that are familiar, to take advantage of knowledge readers already have via metaphor or analogy. However, you want names that are unique, so that others who are also choosing names will not accidentally choose names that interfere with yours.

The first rule I follow is no abbreviations. Abbreviations optimize typing (a 10–100 times in 20 years task) over reading (a 1000–10000 times in 20 years task). Abbreviations make the interpretation of a name a two step process—what do the letters stand for and then what do those words mean. The class and method naming patterns here will produce names that you should never have to abbreviate.

Naming the root class of a large hierarchy is a momentous occasion. People will be using the words you choose in their conversation for the next 20 years. You want to be sure you do it right.

Unfortunately, many people get all formal when they go to name a superclass. Just calling it what it is isn't enough. They have to tack on a flowery, computer science-y, impressive sounding, but ultimately meaningless word, like Object, Thing, Component, Part, Manager, Entity, or Item.

You're creating a vocabulary, not writing a program. Be a poet for a moment. The simple, the punchy, the easily remembered will be far more effective in the long run than some long name that says it all, but in such a way that no one wants to say it at all.

- *Name a superclass with a single word that conveys its purpose in the design.*

Here are some good examples in the image:

Number
Collection
Magnitude
Model

FORWARD

You may create variations on this class, each with a Qualified Subclass Name (p. 169).

Qualified Subclass Name

BACK

You have created a Simple Superclass Name (p. 168).

- What do you name a new subclass?

One way to name classes is to give each a unique name, indicative of its purpose. Unique names give you the opportunity to convey a lot of information without creating names that are long and unwieldy.

This is exactly the right thing to do if the names are in common use. Array is a subclass of Collection because lots of software engineers guess correctly about the nature of the class by reading "Array." Number is a subclass of Magnitude because Number-ness is far more important to communicate than Magnitude-ness. String is a subclass of Collection because everyone knows what a String is.

In general, if I am using inheritance strictly for code sharing, but the role of the subclass is different than the role of the superclass, I go back to Simple Superclass Name.

More often, the inheritance structure of your code is important for a reader to understand, particularly where a subclass is both conceptually a variation on the superclass and they share implementation. The two pieces of information you need to communicate are:

- how the new class is the same; and
- how the new class is different.

You can communicate how the new class is the same by naming some superclass. It need not be the immediate superclass, if some distant ancestor communicates more clearly.

You can communicate how the new class is different by finding a word that accurately highlights the reason the new class isn't just the superclass.

- *Name subclasses in your hierarchies by prepending an adjective to the superclass name.*

For example:

- OrderedCollection is a Collection in which elements are Ordered.

- SortedCollection is a Collection in which elements are Sorted. Even though SortedCollection subclasses OrderedCollection, you wouldn't call it SortedOrderedCollection. The choice to subclass OrderedCollection is strictly for implementation reasons, not because the two collections play similar roles.

- LargeInteger is an Integer that takes many bits to represent.

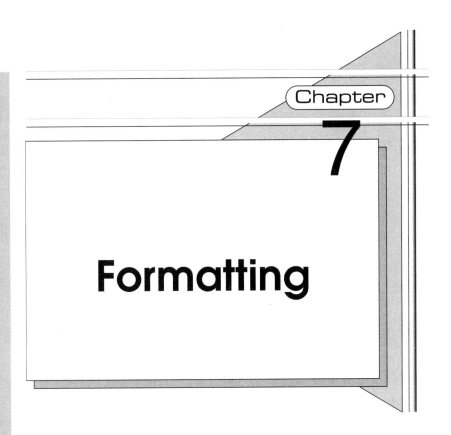

Chapter 7

Formatting

No other topic generates more heat and less light than code formatting. Everybody has their own style and attempts to impose another style are met with ferocious resistance. So, why am I willingly sticking my head into this buzz saw?

The first reason is "because it is there." I want to push patterns to their limit, to see how well they apply to a detail-oriented, exception-ridden, and emotion-filled topic. I wrote these patterns over the course of a couple of months. As new special cases came up, I either had to modify the patterns, add a new pattern, or format my code according to the existing patterns. Before long, I no longer was finding cases where I had to change the patterns. I am quite pleased that all of formatting in Smalltalk fits into ten patterns.

The second reason is "because it is important." Not necessarily formatting code according to these patterns but formatting them according to some set of consistent rules gives a team a smoothness to their interaction. If everybody formats the same way, then reviews and code transfer are never delayed while someone "cleans up" the code. Done right, formatting can convey a lot of information about the structure of code at a glance.

The third reason is to advance the discussion of formatting. Stating the rules as patterns makes my goals and tradeoffs explicit. If you have a different style, you can use these patterns as an example to cast your own rules as patterns. Then you can compare, explicitly, what problems each set of patterns solves and what problems each ignores.

The priorities of these patterns are:

1. To make the gross structure of the method apparent at a glance. Complex messages and blocks, in particular, should jump out at the reader.

2. To preserve vertical space. There is a huge difference between reading a method that fits into the text pane of a browser and reading one that forces you to scroll. Keeping methods compact vertically lets you have smaller browsers and still be able to read methods without scrolling. This reduces window management overhead and leaves more screen space for other programming tools.

3. To be easy to remember. I have seen style guides that have 50–100 rules for formatting. Formatting is important but it shouldn't take that much brain power.

There are many styles of Smalltalk coding for which these formatting patterns would be a disaster. Long methods and methods that use complex expressions look terrible formatted this way. However, thorough use of Composed Method and Explaining Temporary Variable, along with the attitude that you are writing for a reader and not the computer, will go a long way towards helping you produce code that is simple to format and simple to read.

Inline Message Pattern

You are about to write a method for an Intention Revealing Selector (p. 49).

- How do you format the message pattern?

One alternative is to write the keyword/argument pairs one per line. This makes it easy to see what the selector of the method is by reading straight down from the top left corner. However, this style of formatting will often take up three or four lines of vertical space. Composed Methods are generally only a few lines long. It seems a waste of space to have more introduction than content.

Another reason for lining up the keywords vertically is that early text editors did not have line wrapping, so if you wanted to see all the parameters, you had to scroll horizontally. All current Smalltalks have line wrapping available in the source code editor, so all arguments are available regardless of window size or message pattern width.

The problem of reading the selector as a whole is solved by the browser. You never look at a method as a raw piece of text. Methods always appear in the context of a browser. The selector is always presented near the method. If you forget what method you are working on, a quick glance above the method will answer your question.

By saving the vertical space otherwise taken up by the message pattern, you can quickly scan many methods in a smaller browser than is otherwise possible. This allows you to have more information on the screen at the same time, if it is useful. There is a big difference between browsing a program without every having to scroll the text of a method and browsing where you are constantly scrolling.

- *Write the message pattern without explicit line breaks.*

Here is a message pattern formatted with this pattern:

```
from: fromInteger to: toInteger with: aCollection startingAt:
startInteger
```

I've seen this formatted like this:

```
from: fromInteger
to: toInteger
with: aCollection
startingAt: startInteger
```

or worse:

> from: fromInteger
>   to: toInteger
>   with: aCollection
>   startingAt: startInteger

Both of these spend vertical space, increasing the chance that you won't be able to see the body of the method (the part that matters and the part that is likely to be surprising) without scrolling.

Use Type Suggesting Parameter Names (p. 174) for parameters.

Type Suggesting Parameter Name

You are writing an Inline Message Pattern (p. 172). You might be completing a Double Dispatch (p. 55).

- What do you call a method parameter?

There are two important pieces of information associated with every variable—what messages it receives (its type) and what role it plays in the computation. Understanding the type and role of variables is important for understanding a piece of code.

Keywords communicate their associated parameter's role. Since the keywords and parameters are together at the head of every method, the reader can easily understand a parameter's role without any help from the name.

Smalltalk doesn't have a strong notion of types. The set of messages sent to a variable appears nowhere in the language or programming environment. Because of this lack, there is no direct way to communicate types.

Classes sometimes play the role of types. You would expect a Number to be able to respond to messages like +, -, *, and /; or a Collection to do: and includes:.

- *Name parameters according to their most general expected class, preceded by "a" or "an." If there is more than one parameter with the same expected class, precede the class with a descriptive word.*

An Array that requires Integer keys names the parameters to at:put: as

```
at: anInteger put: anObject
```

A Dictionary, where the key can be any object, names the parameters:

```
at: keyObject put: valueObject
```

After you have named the parameters, you are ready to write the method. You may have to declare Role Suggesting Temporary Variable Names (p. 110). You may need to format an Indented Control Flow (p. 175). You may have to use a Guard Clause (p. 178) to protect the execution of the body of the method.

Indented Control Flow

- How do you indent messages?

The conflicting needs of formatting to produce both few lines and short lines is thrown in high relief with this pattern. The only saving grace is that Composed Method creates methods with little enough functionality that you never need to deal with hundreds or thousands of words in a method.

One extreme would be to place all the keywords and arguments on the same line, no matter how long the method. This minimizes the length of the method but makes it difficult to read.

If there are multiple keywords to a message, the fact that they all appear is important to communicate quickly to a scanning reader. By placing each keyword/argument pair on its own line, you can make it easy for the reader to recognize the presence of complex messages.

Arguments do not need to be aligned, unlike keywords, because readers seldom scan all the arguments. Arguments are only interesting in the context of their keyword.

- *Put zero or one argument messages on the same lines as their receiver. For messages with two or more keywords put each keyword/argument pair on its own line, indented one tab.*

Here are some zero and one argument messages formatted with Indented Control Flow:

```
foo isNil
2 + 3
a < b ifTrue: [...]
```

Here are some two argument messages formatted with Indented Control Flow:

```
a < b
    ifTrue: [...]
    ifFalse: [...]
array
    at: 5
    put: #abc
```

Many people have complex exceptions for formatting control statements, like ifTrue: and whileTrue:. One of the things I really like about this pattern is that it gives reasonable results while treating conditional statements as just another message send (which they are, after all).

Formatting code like this makes reading the whole selector easy. You can easily read that the message in this example is #copyFrom:to:with:startingAt:

```
aCollection
    copyFrom: 1
    to: aString size
    with: aString
    startingAt: 1
```

FORWARD

Rectangular Block (p. 177) formats blocks. Guard Clause (p. 178) prevents indent-ing from marching across the page.

BACK

Rectangular Block

You are writing an expression with Indented Control Flow (p. 175).

- How do you format blocks?

Smalltalk distinguishes between code that is executed immediately upon the activation of a method and code whose execution is deferred. To read code accurately, you must be able to quickly distinguish which code in a method falls into which category.

Code should occupy as few lines as possible, consistent with readability. Short methods are easier to assimilate quickly and they fit more easily into a browser. On the other hand, making it easy for the eye to pick out blocks is a reasonable use of extra lines.

One more resource we can bring to bear on this problem is the tendency of the eye to distinguish and interpolate vertical and horizontal lines. The square brackets used to signify blocks lead the eye to create the illusion of a whole rectangle even though one isn't there. Therefore:

- *Make blocks rectangular. Use the square brackets as the upper left and bottom right corners of the rectangle. If the statement in the block is simple, the block can fit on one line. If the statement is compound, bring the block onto its own line and indent.*

Here are a couple of one line blocks:

```
ifTrue: [self recomputeAngle]
ifTrue: [^angle * 90 + 270 degreesToRadians]
```

Here is a block that takes two lines because it contains two statements:

```
ifTrue:
    [self clearCaches.
    self recomputeAngle]
```

Here is a block that takes two lines because it contains a two parameter message:

```
ifTrue:
    [self
        at: each
        put: 0]
```

Guard Clause

You are writing an expression with an Indented Control Flow (p. 175).

How do you format code that shouldn't execute if a condition holds?

In the bad old days of Fortran programming, when it was possible to have multiple entries and exits to a single routine, tracing the flow of control was a nightmare. Which statements in a routine got executed, and when, was impossible to determine statically. This lead to the commandment "Every routine shall have one entry and one exit."

Smalltalk labors under few of the same constraints of long ago Fortran, but the prohibition against multiple exits persists. When routines are only a few lines long, understanding flow of control within a routine is simple. It is the flow between routines that becomes the legitimate focus of attention.

Multiple returns can simplify the formatting of code, particularly conditionals. What's more, the multiple return version of a method is often a more direct expression of the programmer's intent. Therefore:

- *Format the one-branch conditional with an explicit return.*

Let's say you have a method that connects a communication device only if the device isn't already connected. The single exit version of the method might be:

```
connect
        self isConnected
                ifFalse: [self connectConnection]
```

You can read this as "If I am not already connected, connect my connection." The guard clause version of the same method is:

```
connect
        self isConnected ifTrue: [^self].
        self connectConnection
```

You can read this as "Don't do anything if I am connected. Connect my connection." The guard clause is more a statement of fact, or an invariant, than a path of control to be followed.

Conditional Expression

- How do you format conditional expressions where both branches assign or return a value?

Most programming languages make a distinction between statements that work solely by side effect and expressions that return values. For example, control structures in C and Pascal work only by controlling how other statements execute.

In Smalltalk, there are no pure statements. All control structures are implemented in terms of messages, and all messages return values. This leads to the possibility of using the value of control structures.

Programmers new to Smalltalk are likely to be surprised the first time they encounter loops or conditionals used as an expression. New Smalltalkers are likely to write:

```
self isInitialized
    ifTrue: [cost := self calculateCost]
    ifFalse: [cost := 0]
```

These expressions can be translated into the following without changing the meaning:

```
cost := self isInitialized
    ifTrue: [self calculateCost]
    ifFalse: [0]
```

Is the simpler form worth the possibility of confusion for beginners? It more directly communicates the intent of the expression. You don't mean "There are two paths of expression, one of which sets the value of cost to the result of sending myself calculateCost and the other of which sets the value of cost to 0." You mean, "Set cost to one of two values, either the result of sending myself calculateCost or 0."

- *Format conditionals so their value is used where it clearly express-es the intent of the method.*

Assignment and return are often found in both branches of a con-ditional. Look for opportunities to factor both to the outside of the conditional.

Here is an example of a return on both branches of a conditional:

```
cost
        self isInitialized
                ifTrue: [^self calculateCost]
                ifFalse: [^0]
```

If I write code like this, I don't mean, "Here are two alternative paths of execution." I mean, "Here are two alternative values to be returned." Thus, a Conditional Expression expresses my intent more clearly:

```
cost
        ^self isInitialized
                ifTrue: [self calculateCost]
                ifFalse: [0]
```

I commonly see code in which both sides of a conditional expres-sion evaluate to a Boolean. Start with this:

```
aCollection isEmpty
        ifTrue: [empty := true]
        ifFalse: [empty := false]
```

Using Conditional Expression we first factor out the assignment:

```
empty := aCollection isEmpty
    ifTrue: [true]
    ifFalse: [false]
```

We can go a step further and eliminate the conditional entirely. The following code is equivalent to the preceding:

```
empty := aCollection isEmpty
```

BACK

You may be able to express one or both branches of the conditional more explicitly by using a Composed Method (p. 21).

Simple Enumeration Parameter

- What do you call the parameter to an enumeration block?

It is tempting to try to pack as much meaning as possible into every name. Certainly, classes, instance variables, and messages deserve careful attention. Each of these elements can communicate volumes about your intent as you program.

Some variables just don't deserve such attention. Variables that are always used the same way, where their meaning can be easily understood from context, call for consistency over creativity. The effort to carefully name such variables is wasted because no non-obvious information is communicated to the program. They may even be counter productive, if the reader tries to impute meaning to the variable that isn't there.

- *Call the parameter "each." If you have nested enumeration blocks, append a descriptive word to all parameter names.*

For example, the meaning of "each" in

```
self children do: [:each | self processChild: each]
```

is clear. If the block is more complicated, each may not be descriptive enough. In that case, you should invoke Composed Method to turn the block into a single message. The Type Suggesting Parameter in the new method will clarify the meaning of the object.

The typical example of nested blocks is iterating over the two dimensions of a bitmap:

```
1 to: self width do:
    [:eachX |
    1 to: self height do:
        [:eachY | ...]]
```

Nested blocks that iterate over unlike collections should probably be factored with Composed Method.

You may need Composed Method to simplify the enumeration block.

Cascade

- How do you format multiple messages to the same receiver?

The simplest solution is to just repeat the expression that created the receiver. Such code looks like this:

```
self listPane parent color: Color black.
self listPane parent height: 17.
self listPane parent width: 11.
```

For complex expressions, the first simplification is to use an Explaining Temporary Variable to hold the value of the expression:

```
| parent |
parent := self listPane parent.
parent color: Color black.
parent height: 17.
parent width: 11.
```

One of Smalltalk's few syntactic quirks is a solution to this problem. Rather than having to repeat an expression or create a temporary variable to hold the expression, Smalltalk lets you say at the end of one message "Here's another message to the same receiver."

• *Use a Cascade to send several messages to the same receiver. Separate the messages with a semicolon. Put each message on its own line and indent one tab. Only use Cascades for messages with zero or one argument.*

The code above becomes:

```
self listPane parent
        color: Color black;
        height: 17;
        width: 11
```

Whether or not you use a Cascade is really a matter of intent. If you want to communicate "Here are a bunch of messages all going to the same object," that's a good time to use a Cascade. If you just happen to be sending messages to the same object, but it's not really part of the essence of the code that the two messages are going to the same object, don't use a Cascade.

One confusion that sometimes arises about Cascade is if the initial expression is complex, where do the cascaded messages get sent?

For example, in:

```
OrderedCollection new
        add: 5;
        add: 10
```

the indentation cues you that both adds get sent to the new OrderedCollection, not the class itself. Here's the rule: All subsequent messages in a Cascade go to the same receiver as the first message in the cascade (in this case, #add:). Any preceding parts of the expression that got you the receiver are irrelevant.

The restriction that Cascades only be used with zero or one argument messages comes from the difficulty in visually parsing Cascades with varying numbers of arguments. In the example above, what if you could send height:width: as a single message? Using Cascade, the code would look like:

```
self listPane parent
        color: Color black;
        height: 17
        width: 11
```

At a glance, you can't tell whether height and width are set separately or together. The readability gains of a Cascade are quickly lost if you have to spend any time figuring out the messages that are sent. Fortunately, most times messages go to the same receiver (especially more than two), the messages are simple.

You may have to use Yourself (p. 186) if you are using the value of a Cascade.

Yourself

You need to use the value of a Cascade (p. 183).

- How can you use the value of a Cascade if the last message doesn't return the receiver of the message?

This has got to be the number one confusing method in all of Smalltalk. There it is in Object, where every new Smalltalker stumbles across it:

```
Object>>yourself
    ^self
```

Or, if the programmer was really clever (and didn't know about Interesting Return Value):

```
Object>>yourself
```

What's going on?

Let's say you want to add a bunch of elements to an OrderedCollection. Collection>>add: anObject is defined to return anObject, not the receiver of the message. If you want to assign the Collection to a variable:

```
all := OrderedCollection new
        add: 5;
        add: 7
```

will result in the value of all being 7. There are two solutions to this problem. The first is to put the variable assignment in parentheses:

```
(all := OrderedCollection new)
        add: 5;
        add: 7
```

- *When you need the value of a Cascade and the last message does not return the receiver, append the message "yourself" to the Cascade.*

Our example becomes:

```
all := OrderedCollection new
        add: 5;
        add: 7;
        yourself
```

Sending "yourself" returns the receiver, the new instance of OrderedCollection. That's the object that gets assigned to the variable.

I've seen folks become defensive about "yourself," tacking it onto every Cascade they write. You shouldn't do this. "yourself" is there to communicate to your reader that you really want the value of the receiver used, not the result of sending a message. If you aren't using the value of a Cascade, don't use "yourself." For example, I wouldn't use it in Point>>printOn:, because I don't assign the value of the Cascade to a variable or return it as the value of the method.

```
Point>>printOn: aStream
    aStream
        print: self x;
        nextPut: $@;
        print: self y
```

Having written this, I'm not sure why I prefer Cascades to the parenthesized format. Perhaps it's because there is a big psychological difference in parsing a method with parentheses and one without. If I can avoid parentheses and still have a method that reads clearly, I will.

Another use of "yourself" is with #inject:into:. Suppose you want to put all the children of a collection of parents together in a Set. You might be tempted to write:

```
parents
    inject: Set new
    into: [:sum :each | sum addAll: each children]
```

But this wouldn't work because the result of sending #addAll: is the argument (in this case the children), not the receiver. To get this to work as expected, you have to write:

```
parents
    inject: Set new
    into: [:sum :each | sum addAll: each children; yourself]
```

Interesting Return Value

- When do you explicitly return a value at the end of a method?

All messages return a value. If a method does not explicitly return a value, the receiver of the message is returned by default. This causes some confusion for new programmers, who may be used to Pascal's distinction between procedures and functions, or C's lack of a definition of the return value of a procedure with no explicit return. To compensate, some programmers always explicitly return a value from every method.

The distinction between methods that do their work by side effect and those that are valuable for the result they return is important. An unfamiliar reader wanting to quickly understand the expected use of a method should be able to glance at the last line and instantly understand whether a useful return value is generated or not. Therefore:

- *Return a value only when you intend for the sender to use the value.*

For example, consider the implementation of topComponent in VisualWorks. Visual components form a tree, with a ScheduledWindow at the root. Any component in the tree can fetch the root by sending itself the message "topComponent." VisualPart (the superclass of interior nodes and leaves) implements this message by asking the container for its topComponent:

```
VisualPart>>topComponent
    ^container topComponent
```

ScheduledWindow implements the base case of the recursion by returning itself. The simplest implementation would be to have a method with no statements. It would return the receiver. However, using Interesting Return Value, because the result is intended to be used by the sender, it explicitly returns "self."

```
ScheduledWindow>>topComponent
    ^self
```

Chapter

8

Development Example

In this chapter, I will pretend to develop a piece of software guided by the Best Practice Patterns. It will likely seem incredibly slow to you, since I won't write more than a couple of words of code without pointing out another pattern. Not to worry, once you get used to the patterns you don't really think of them individually. You build higher levels of structure in your mind that let you just write clean code quickly and without thinking consciously of the smaller steps, much as you can speak without consulting a grammar book.

Problem

The problem we will solve is representing multi-currency monetary values. It's not as simple as it might seem. There are lots of unit-value computations in the world. Any time you use a number, you generally have at least an implied set of units behind it, whether inches, pixels, or kilograms. Some units can be freely converted into others, like pounds to kilograms. Others just don't make any sense. If you add four meters to two grams you should get an error. One simplifying assumption that makes unit-values easy to program is that for conversions that make sense, there is a single, immutable conversion ratio. You don't have to go look up the New York spot quote on pound to kilograms every morning.

Money is different. There is no single conversion rate. There isn't really a single sequence of conversion rates. Sometimes, you want to answer questions like, "How does the value of my portfolio differ if I liquidate it in Hong Kong or Zurich?" This need for flexibility is the primary driving force in designing objects to represent currency.

Start

The first object we'll give the Simple Superclass Name of Money. It represents a value in a single currency.

```
Class: Money
    superclass: Object
    instance variables: amount currency
```

The variable with the Role Suggesting Instance Variable Name "amount" will hold any old Number. This lets us defers issues of numerical accuracy and stability to the Number classes. If you want a super accurate but slow Money, you can make the Amount a FixedPoint. If you want less accuracy but more speed, you can use a Double. As long as the amount responds to number-like messages, Money won't care.

The variable "currency" will hold Symbol for now, the name of a currency. Currency traders use standard three letter abbreviations for the currencies of the world—USD for United States Dollars, for example. A complete currency system needs a real Currency object, because different currencies act different computationally, but for now all we care about is whether two currencies are equal or not.

How do we create a Money? We need a Constructor Method.

```
Money class>>amount: aNumber currency: aSymbol
    ^self new
        setAmount: aNumber
        currency: aSymbol
```

The method communicates the types of its parameters with Type Suggesting Parameter Names. The body of the method uses Indented Control Flow to make it clear to the reader that the Constructor Parameter Method takes two arguments. Constructor Methods also always have an Interesting Return Value.

Now we need to set the instance variables to the objects provided to the Constructor Method. We write a Constructor Parameter Method:

```
Money>>setAmount: aNumber currency: aSymbol
    amount := aNumber.
    currency := aSymbol
```

If we want to check that our code works, we will need a Debug Print Method.

```
Money>>printOn: aStream
    aStream
        print: amount;
        space;
        nextPutAll: currency
```

Note that this method uses a Cascade to show that three message are being sent to the same Stream.

Now we can try out the code in a workspace (the stuff in italics is what prints as a result):

```
Money
    amount: 5
    currency: #USD 5 USD
```

Arithmetic

How do we add two Moneys together? Let's get the simple case right first, where we have the same currency in both Moneys. When you add two Moneys with the same currency together, the resulting Money should have as its amount the sum of the amounts of the first two.

```
Money>>+ aMoney
    ^self species
        amount: amount + aMoney amount
        currency: currency
```

We need a Getting Method for the variable "amount" for this to work:

```
Money>>amount
    ^amount
```

We get the right answer if we're adding dollars to dollars:

```
| m1 m2 |
m1 := Money
        amount: 5
        currency: #USD.
m2 := Money
        amount: 7
        currency: #USD.
m1 + m2 12 USD
```

Change one of the Moneys to a different currency, though, and we get the wrong answer:

```
| m1 m2 |
m1 := Money
        amount: 5
        currency: #USD.
m2 := Money
        amount: 7
        currency: #GBP.
m1 + m2 12 USD
```

Five dollars and seven pounds is not twelve dollars. How are we going to keep the simple "+" protocol for arithmetic and still handle the case where we have multiple currencies? The answer is to introduce an Impostor (a modeling pattern) for a Money that defers exchange rate conversions. We'll give it the Simple Superclass Name of MoneySum.

```
Class: MoneySum
        superclass: Object
        instance variables: monies
```

The variable with the Role Suggesting Instance Variable Name "monies" will hold a Collection of Moneys.

We create a MoneySum with a Constructor Method:

```
MoneySum class>>monies: aCollection
    ^self new setMonies: aCollection
```

The collection is passed on to the Constructor Parameter Method:

```
MoneySum>>setMonies: aCollection
    monies := aCollection
```

We'll add a Debug Print Method to MoneySum so we can check our results:

```
MoneySum>>printOn: aStream
    monies do:
        [:each |
        aStream
            print: each;
            nextPutAll: ' + '].
    aStream skip: -3
```

We used a basketful of patterns in this method: Direct Variable Access, Role Suggesting Parameter Name, Simple Enumeration Parameter, Rectangular Block, Indented Control Flow, and Do.

With MoneySum in hand, we can modify Money>>+ to return a MoneySum if the two currencies don't match:

```
Money>>+ aMoney
      ^currency = aMoney currency
            ifTrue:
                  [self species
                        amount: amount + aMoney amount
                        currency: currency]
            ifFalse:
                  [MoneySum monies: (Array
                        with: self
                        with: aMoney)]
```

We need a Getting Method for Money's currency:

```
Money>>currency
      ^currency
```

Now our multi-currency example works:

```
| m1 m2 |
m1 := Money
      amount: 5
      currency: #USD.
m2 := Money
      amount: 7
      currency: #GBP.
m1 + m2 5 USD + 7 GBP
```

Just to check, the single currency example works, still:

```
| m1 m2 |
m1 := Money
    amount: 5
    currency: #USD.
m2 := Money
    amount: 7
    currency: #USD.
m1 + m2  12 USD
```

Integration

For a MoneySum to truly be an Impostor for a Money, it has to support all the same messages. All the combinations of Moneys and MoneySums have to work together. We will use Double Dispatch to implement this. Double Dispatch states: "Send a message to the argument. Append the class name of the receiver to the selector. Pass the receiver as an argument." Money addition becomes:

```
Money>> + aMoney
    ^aMoney addMoney: self
```

The old Money>>+ becomes Money>>addMoney:

```
Money>>addMoney: aMoney
    ^currency = aMoney currency
        ifTrue:
            [self species
                amount: amount + aMoney amount
                currency: currency]
        ifFalse:
            [MoneySum monies: (Array
                with: self
                with: aMoney)]
```

MoneySum arithmetic follows the Double Dispatch pattern, too:

```
MoneySum>> + aMoney
    ^aMoney addMoneySum: self
```

If a MoneySum is adding a Money, it should produce a new MoneySum with the Money added to the list of Monies:

```
MoneySum>>addMoney: aMoney
    ^self species monies: (monies copyWith: aMoney)
```

Now we can send "+" to a Money with a MoneySum as argument:

```
| m1 m2 |
m1 := Money
        amount: 5
        currency: #USD.
m2 := Money
        amount: 7
        currency: #GBP.
m1 + (m2 + m1) 5 USD + 7 GBP + 5 USD
```

To complete the Double Dispatch, we have to implement addMoneySum: in Money and MoneySum. The implementation in Money is simple, we just turn around and send addMoney: to the MoneySum, trusting the existing implementation to work:

```
Money>> addMoneySum: aMoneySum
    ^aMoneySum addMoney: self
```

We can test this:

```
| m1 m2 |
m1 := Money
        amount: 5
        currency: #USD.
m2 := Money
        amount: 7
        currency: #GBP.
m1 + m2 + m1 7 GBP + 5 USD + 5 USD
```

The final combination is adding a MoneySum to a MoneySum. We do this by concatenating the monies of both of them:

```
MoneySum>>addMoneySum: aMoneySum
        ^MoneySum monies: monies , aMoneySum monies
```

We can test this:

```
| m1 m2 |
m1 := Money
        amount: 5
        currency: #USD.
m2 := Money
        amount: 7
        currency: #GBP.
(m1 + m2) + (m1 + m2) 7 GBP + 5 USD + 7 GBP + 5 USD
```

Summary

We used these patterns in the code above:

Pattern	Example
Simple Superclass Name	Money, MoneySum
Constructor Method	MoneySum class>>monies:
Constructor Parameter Method	MoneySum>>setMonies:
Common State, Role Suggesting Instance Variable Name	Money "currency"
Intention Revealing Selector	Money>>+
Getting Method	Money>>currency
Composed Method	Money class>>amount:currency:
Decomposing Message	Money class>>amount:currency: sending #setAmount:currency:
Choosing Message	addMoney:, addMoneySum:
Dispatched Interpretation, Double Dispatch	Money>>addMoney:
Debug Print Method	Money>>printOn:
Array	MoneySum
Inline Message Pattern	Money>>setAmount:currency:
Indented Control Flow	Money>>addMoney:
Conditional Expression	Money>>addMoney:
Rectangular Block	Money>>addMoney:
Direct Variable Access	Money>>addMoney:
Type Suggesting Parameter Name	Money class>>amount: aNumber currency: aSymbol
Simple Enumeration Parameter	MoneySum>>printOn:
Interesting Return Value	Money>>addMoney:

As you can see from this list, even simple code uses many different techniques to communicate to readers.

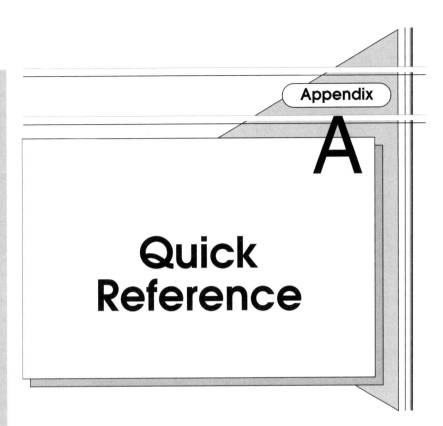

Quick Reference

Composed Method	How do you divide a program into methods?	Divide your program into methods that perform one identifiable task. Keep all of the operations in a method at the same level of abstraction. This will naturally result in programs with many small methods, each a few lines long.
Constructor Method	How do you represent instance creation?	Provide methods that create well-formed instances. Pass all required parameters to them.
Constructor Parameter Method	How do you set instance variables from the parameters to a Constructor Method?	Code a single method that sets all the variables. Preface its name with "set", then the names of the variables.

Shortcut Constructor Method	What is the external interface for creating a new object when a Constructor Method is too wordy?	Represent object creation as a message to one of the arguments to the Constructor Method. Add no more than three of these Shortcut Constructor Methods per system you develop.
Conversion	How do you convert information from one object's format to another's?	Convert from one object to another rather than over-whelm any one object's protocol.
Converter Method	How do you represent simple conversion of an object to another object with the same protocol but different format?	Provide a method in the object to be converted that converts to the new object. Name the method by prepending "as" to the class of the object returned.
Converter Constructor Method	How do you represent the conversion of an object to another with a different protocol?	Make a Constructor Method that takes the object to be converted as an argument.
Query Method	How do you represent testing a property of an object?	Provide a method that returns a Boolean. Name it by prefacing the property name with a form of "be"—is, was, will, etc.
Comparing Method	How do you order objects with respect to each other?	Implement "<=" to return true if the receiver should be ordered before the argument.
Reversing Method	How do you code a smooth flow of messages?	Code a method on the parameter. Derive its name from the original message. Take the original receiver as a parameter to the new method. Implement the method by sending the original message to the original receiver.

Method Object	How do you code a method where many lines of code share many arguments and temporary variables?	Create an class named after the method. Give it an instance variable for the receiver of the original method, each argument, and each temporary variable. Give it a Constructor Method that takes the original receiver and the method arguments. Give it one instance method, #compute, implemented by copying the body of the original method. Replace the method with one which creates an instance of the new class and sends it #compute.
Execute Around Method	How do you represent pairs of actions that have to be taken together?	Code a method that takes a Block as an argument. Name the method by appending "During: aBlock" to the name of the first method that needs to be invoked. In the body of the Execute Around Method, invoke the first method, evaluate the block, then invoke the second method.
Debug Printing Method	How do you code the default printing method?	Override printOn: to provide information about an object's structure to the programmer.
Method Comment	How do you comment methods?	Communicate important information that is not obvious from the code in a comment at the beginning of the method.
Message	How do you invoke computation?	Send a named message and let the receiving object decide what to do with it.

Choosing Message	How do you execute one of several alternatives?	Send a message to one of several different kinds of objects, each of which executes one alternative.
Decomposing Message	How do you invoke parts of a computation?	Send several messages to "self."
Intention Revealing Message	How do you communicate your intent when the implementation is simple?	Send a message to "self." Name the message so it communicates what is to be done rather than how it is to be done. Code a simple method for the message.
Intention Revealing Selector	What do you name a method?	Name methods after what they accomplish.
Dispatched Interpretation	How can two objects cooperate when one wishes to conceal its representation?	Have the client send a message to the encoded object. Pass a parameter to which the encoded object will send decoded messages.
Double Dispatch	How can you code a computation that has many cases, the cross product of two families of classes?	Send a message to the argument. Append the class name of the receiver to the selector. Pass the receiver as an argument.
Mediating Protocol	How do you code the interaction between two objects that need to remain independent?	Refine the protocol between the objects so the words used are consistent.
Super	How can you invoke super class behavior?	Invoke code in a super class explicitly by sending a message to "super" instead of "self." The method corresponding to the message will be found in the super class of the class implementing the sending method.
Extending Super	How do you add to a super class' implementation of a method?	Override the method and send a message to "super" in the overriding method.

Modifying Super	How do you change part of the behavior of a super class' method without modifying it?	Override the method and invoke "super", then execute the code to modify the results.
Delegation	How does an object share implementation without inheritance?	Pass part of its work on to another object.
Simple Delegation	How do you invoke a disinterested delegate?	Delegate messages unchanged.
Self Delegation	How do you implement delegation to an object that needs reference to the delegating object?	Pass along the delegating object (i.e. "self") in an additional parameter called "for:."
Pluggable Behavior	How do you parameterize the behavior of an object?	Add a variable that will be used to trigger different behavior.
Pluggable Selector	How do you code simple instance specific behavior?	Add a variable that contains a selector to be performed. Append "Message" to the Role Suggesting Instance Variable Name. Create a Composed Method that simply performs the selector.
Pluggable Block	How do you code complex Pluggable Behavior that is not quite worth its own class?	Add an instance variable to store a Block. Append "Block" to the Role Suggesting Instance Variable Name. Create a Composed Method to evaluate the Block to invoke the Pluggable Behavior.
Collecting Parameter	How do you return a collection that is the collaborative result of several methods?	Add a parameter that collects their results to all of the submethods.
Common State	How do you represent state, different values for which will exist in all instances of a class?	Declare an instance variable in the class.

Variable State	How do you represent state whose presence varies from instance to instance?	Put variables that only some instances will have in a Dictionary stored in an instance variable called "properties." Implement "propertyAt: aSymbol" and "propertyAt:aSymbol put: anObject" to access properties.
Explicit Initialization	How do you initialize instance variables to their default value?	Implement a method "initialize" that sets all the values explicitly. Override the class message new to invoke it on new instances.
Lazy Initialization	How do you initialize an instance variable to its default value?	Write a Getting Method for the variable. Initialize it if necessary with a Default Value Method.
Default Value Method	How do you represent the default value of a variable?	Create a method that returns the value. Prepend "default" to the name of the variable as the name of the method.
Constant Method	How do you code a constant?	Create a method that returns the constant.
Direct Variable Access	How do you get and set an instance variable's value?	Access and set the variable directly.
Indirect Variable Access	How do you get and set an instance variable's value?	Access and set its value only through a Getting Method and Setting Method.
Getting Method	How do you provide access to an instance variable?	Provide a method that returns the value of the variable. Give it the same name as the variable.
Setting Method	How you change the value of an instance variable?	Provide a method with the same name as the variable. Have it take a single parameter, the value to be set.

Collection Accessor Method	How do you provide access to an instance variable that holds a collection?	Provide methods that are implemented with Delegation to the collection. To name the methods, add the name of the collection to the collection messages.
Enumeration Method	How do you provide safe, general access to collection elements?	Implement a method that executes a Block for each element of the collection. Name the method by concatenating the name of the collection and "Do:."
Boolean Property Setting Method	How do you set a boolean property?	Create two methods beginning with "be." One has property name, the other the negation. Add "toggle" if the client doesn't want to know about the current state.
Role Suggesting Instance Variable Name	What do you name an instance variable?	Name instance variables for the role they play in the computation. Make the name plural if the variable will hold a Collection.
Temporary Variable	How do you save the value of an expression for later use within a method?	Create a variable whose scope and extent is a single method. Declare it just below the method selector. Assign it as soon as the expression is valid.
Collecting Temporary Variable	How do you gradually collect values to be used later in a method?	When you need to collect or merge objects over a complex enumeration, use a temporary variable to hold the collection or merged value.
Caching Temporary Variable	How do you improve the performance of a method?	Set a temporary variable to the value of the expression as soon as it is valid. Use the variable instead of the expression in the remainder of the method.

Explaining Temporary Variable	How do you simplify a complex expression within a method?	Take a subexpression out of the complex expression. Assign its value to a temporary variable before the complex expression. Use the variable instead in the complex expression.
Reusing Temporary Variable	How do you use an expression several places in a method when its value may change?	Execute the expression once and set a temporary variable. Use the variable instead of the expression in the remainder of the method.
Role Suggesting Temporary Variable Name	What do you call a temporary variable?	Name a temporary variable for the role it plays in the computation.
Collection	How do you represent a one-to-many relationship?	Use a Collection.
Ordered Collection	How do you code Collections whose size can't be determined when they are created?	Use an Ordered Collection as your default dynamically sized Collection.
Run Array	How do you compactly code an Ordered Collection or Array where you have the same element many times in a row?	Use a Run Array to compress long runs of the same element.
Set	How do you code a Collection whose elements are unique?	Use a Set.
Equality Method	How do you code equality for new objects?	If you will be putting objects in a Set, using them as Dictionary keys, or otherwise using them with other objects that define equality, define a method called "=." Protect the implementation of "=" so only objects of compatible classes will be fully tested for equality.
Hashing Method	How do you ensure that new objects work correctly with hashed Collections?	If you override "=" and use the object with a hashed Collection, override "hash"

		so that two objects that are equal return the same hash value.
Dictionary	How do you map one kind of object to another?	Use a Dictionary.
Sorted Collection	How do you sort a collection?	Use a Sorted Collection. Set its sort block if you want to sort by some criteria other than"<=."
Array	How do you code a collection with a fixed number of elements? "new:anInteger" so that it	Use an Array. Create it with has space for the number of elements you know it needs.
Byte Array	How do you code an Array of numbers in the range 0..255 or -128..127?	Use a Byte Array.
Interval	How do you code a collection of numbers in sequence?	Use an Interval with start, stop, and an optional step value. The Shortcut Constructor Methods Number>>to: and to:by: build Intervals for you.
Is Empty	How do you test if a collection is empty?	Send is Empty to test whether a collection is empty (has no elements). Use not Empty to test whether a collection has elements.
Includes:	How do you search for a particular element in a collection?	Send includes: and pass the object to be searched for.
Concatentation	How do you put two collections together?	Concatenate two collections by sending "," to the first with the second as an argument.
Enumeration	How do you execute code across a collection?	Use the enumeration messages to spread a com-

putation across a collection.

Do	How do you execute code for each element in a collection?	Send do: to a collection to iterate over its elements. Send a one argument block as the argument to do:. It will be evaluated once for each element.
Collect	How do you operate on the result of a message sent to each object in the collection?	Use collect: to create a new collection whose elements are the results of evaluating the block passed to collect: with each element of the original collection. Use the new collection.
Select/Reject	How do you filter out part of a collection?	Use select: and reject: to return new collections containing only elements of interest. Enumerate the new collection. Both take a one argument Block that returns a Boolean. Select: gives you elements for which the Block returns true, reject: gives you elements for which the Block returns false.
Detect	How do you search a collection?	Search a collection by sending it detect:. The first element for which the block argument evaluates to true will be returned.
Inject:into:	How do you keep a running value as you iterate over a Collection?	Use inject:into: to keep a running value. Make the first argument the initial value. Make the second argument a two-element block. Call the block arguments "sum" and "each." Have the block evaluate to the next value of the

running value.

Duplicate Removing Set	How do you remove the duplicates from a Collection?	Send "asSet" to the Collection. The result will have all duplicates removed.
Temporarily Sorted Collection	How do you present a Collection with one of many sort orders?	Return a sorted copy of the Collection by sending "asSortedCollection" to the Collection. Send "asSortedCollection: aBlock" for custom sort orders.
Stack	How do you implement a stack?	Implement a Stack using an Ordered Collection.
Queue	How do you implement a queue?	Implement queues using an Ordered Collection.
Searching Literal	How do you search for one of a few literal objects known when you write the code?	Ask a literal Collection if it includes the element you are seeking.
Lookup Cache	How do you optimize complex Detect or Select/Reject loops?	Prepend "lookup" to the name of the expensive search or filter method. Add an instance variable holding a Dictionary to cache results. Name the variable by appending "Cache" to the name of the search. Make the parameters of the search the keys of the Dictionary and the results of the search the values.
Parsing Stream	How do you write a simple parser?	Put the Stream in an instance variable. Have all parsing methods work from the same Stream.
Concatenating Stream	How do you concatenate several Collections?	Use a Stream to concatenate many Collections.
Simple Superclass Name	What do you call a class that is expected to be the root of an	Name a superclass with a single word that conveys its

	inheritance hierarchy?	purpose in the design.
Qualified Subclass Name	What do you name a new subclass?	Name subclasses in your hierarchies by prepending an adjective to the super-class name.
Inline Message Pattern	How do you format the message pattern?	Write the message pattern without explicit line breaks.
Type Suggesting Parameter Name	What do you call a method parameter?	Name parameters according to their most general expected class, preceded by "a"or "an." If there is more than one parameter with the same expected class,pre-cede the class with a descriptive word.
Indented Control Flow	How do you indent messages?	Put zero or one argument messages on the same lines as their receiver. For messages with two or more keywords put each key word/argument pair on its own line, indented one tab.
Rectangular Block	How do you format blocks?	Make blocks rectangular. Use the square brackets as the upper left and bottom right corners of the rectangle. If the statement in the block is simple, the block can fit on one line. If the state-ment is compound, bring the block onto its own line and indent.
Guard Clause	How do you format code that shouldn't execute if a condition holds?	Format the one-branch conditional with an explicit return.
Conditional Expression	How do you format conditional expressions where both branches assign or return a value?	Format conditionals so their value is used where it clearly expresses the intent of the method.

Simple Enumeration Parameter	What do you call the parameter to an enumeration block?	Call the parameter "each." If you have nested enumeration blocks, append a descriptive word to all parameter names.
Cascade	How do you format multiple messages to the same receiver?	Use a Cascade to send several messages to the same receiver. Separate the messages with a semicolon. Put each message on its own line and indent one tab. Only use Cascades for messages with zero or one argument.
Yourself	How can you use the value of a Cascade if the last message doesn't return the receiver of the message?	When you need the value of a Cascade and the last message does not return the receiver, append the message "yourself" to the Cascade.
Interesting Return Value	When do you explicitly return a value at the end of a method?	Return a value only when you intend for the sender to use the value.

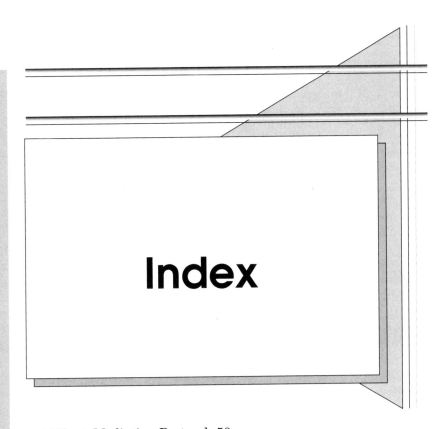

Index